EARTH WORKS

Ceremonies in Tower Time

H. BYRON BALLARD

Smith Bridge Press

ASHEVILLE, NC

Edited by D. A. Sarac
www.TheEditingPen.com

Cover Design by Susan A. McBride
www.SusanMcbrideDesign.com

Contact author at:
Asheville's Village Witch
www.myvillagewitch.com

ISBN-13: 978-0-9967583-7-6

Smith Bridge Press
Asheville, NC
smithbridgepress@gmail.com

www.SkyeBridgePublishing.com

Dedication

This book has been a decade in the writing and is dedicated to everyone who listened to my mad ramblings about Tower Time and challenged me when I needed it. It is for the Ancestors and the old hills and valleys of the homeland. It is for the scarred, creased, and holy Elders who knew a thing or two about living life in a hard world—may we be blessed with such knowledge in time to make a difference.

A vast old religion, which once swayed the earth, lingers in our senses: a religion in which the whole life-effort was to get our lives into direct contact with the elemental life of the cosmos—mountain-life, cloud-life, thunder-life, air-life, earth-life, sun-life—to come into the immediate felt contact, and so derive energy, power, and joy.

—D.H. Lawrence

Acknowledgments

Special thanks to the home team—Kate (even though she refuses to quit her job and come home) and Joe (who has finally learned not to stand behind me while I'm on the computer): my work-wives Star Bustamonte and Lisa Anderson Svencicki; Annie Sarac and Smith Bridge Press; that Peregrinating Shenanigator Oriana; Asheville Raven and Crone; Asheville GreenWorks; Jesse Israel Garden Center; the Buncombe County Agricultural Extension office; Diotima Mantineia at Urania's Well—www.uraniaswell.com; Diana Cerce, Joan Chesick, and all the Alewives, past and future; the Pagan-friendly UUCSV; Joanna Macy, Starhawk, John Michael Greer and James Lovelock for thought provocation; Darcel Eddins; Organic Growers School and Lee Warren; Southeast Wise Woman Herbal Conference; Incredible Edible Todmorden; Asheville Community Gardens network; Kate O'Connor; Alicia and Gomez; Amanda Strawderman; my beta readers (Alice Rain, Cari Ferraro, Diotima); and to Yoko for love, poetry and coffee.

Portions of this book previously appeared at *The Wild Hunt*, Witches and Pagans magazine and on Facebook; sections from sermons at Unitarian Universalist congregations throughout the South are also used in the essays for each chapter. The "Tower Time Documents File" first appeared on Byron's blog at myvillagewitch.com.

Brian Henke's poem "Love Song for Terra" and lyrics from "Man in the Moon" are used with permission (www.brianhenkeguitarist.com).

Beth Phipps' poem in honor of Bonnie Frontino also appears with the poet's permission.

Kate O'Connor's poem "Crone Song" is used with permission from the author.

Byron Ballard never disappoints her readers, her work is always well researched, and her writing style is always interesting and chock-full of sage insights. Her in-person workshops are always well attended at FPG, and the comment cards all come back to us with glowing reviews of the high caliber of the class.
—*Ann Marie Augustino, President, Florida Pagan Gathering*

Earth Works isn't just another book about nature-based magic and spirituality, it's a profound and much-needed survival guide for the times we live in. With a conversational yet no-nonsense tone, Byron firmly beckons us to examine our world and our connection to it, physically and spiritually. Seeded with a mixture of anecdotes, rituals, and practical, accessible advice, the reader is provided with tools to not only survive the Tower Times but to grow and flourish beyond them in mind, body, and spirit.
—*Laura Tempest Zakroff, author of Sigil Witchery: A Witch's Guide to Crafting Magick Symbols and The Witch's Cauldron: The Craft, Lore, and Magick of Ritual Vessels*

Byron Ballard's perspective is like witch hazel. It is astringent, fresh, cleansing, and healing.
—*Meg Barnhouse, Senior Minister, First Unitarian Universalist Church of Austin*

If ever there was a book worthy of your time, it would undoubtedly be Byron Ballard's Earth Works. A step-by-step handbook that's not only designed to help us survive the chaos and upheaval in today's world but offers real solutions to restore stability, safety, and security. Putting its solutions into practice will change your life. It will change your community. It even has the power to change the world. And it all begins with reading this book!
—*Dorothy Morrison, Author of The Craft and Utterly Wicked*

This is a book for our times. Byron Ballard profoundly captures the how and why of magical and spiritual dedication to the earth as a way forward toward a global sustainable future. Her writing is both sophisticated and colloquial, bringing a practical reality and an intelligence to a very current topic. At times a sermon and at other times a personal reflection, Earth Works serves as an inspiration, a guidepost, and a call to action for both magical people and others that feel the Earth calling. —*Heather Greene, Managing Editor of The Wild Hunt, author, journalist, film historian, mother, citizen of the planet, witch*

This book is a balm for the weary spirit and the quiet revolution that might just save the planet. —*Kate Laity, Witches & Pagans' History Witch*

I have always appreciated Byron's no-nonsense approach to most things, including I believe her most famous quote to date: "Ain't you people got no gods to worship? No holy days to celebrate? No ancestors to deal with—er, I mean venerate? In short—don't you people have some sacred work to do? Justice work? Environmental work? Community weaving?" This book addresses these questions; delivered with a side of Southern sass and grace and grounded firmly within the context of our post-modern reality. Her invitation to examine our circles of connection (to place, people, resources, magic, etc.) seems at once absurdly simple and yet, like a basic spiritual practice, forms the foundation of deeply meaningful experience and personal formation. I feel the content shared within is valuable not because it's being written for a particular moment in time, for "Tower Time," but because it weaves together so many aspects of the tapestry that represents how we got here, and how do we move forward purposefully and together. —*Rev. Tiffany Andes, Military Circles Program Coordinator, Lady Liberty League Military Affairs*

Pure and simple, Byron Ballard is a force of nature. Her words bring strength enough to take down the walls of oppression brick by bloody brick and rebuild our hearts anew. This newest book of hers, *Earth Works: Ceremonies in Tower Time* is less a

primer on adapting to an ever-turning world and more of a demand for us all to stand at the base of the Tower and cry into the howling storm, "No more!" The reckoning has come and the revolution is at our doorsteps. It is time to kick it down, witches!
—*Tara Maguire, author and podcaster*

For years Byron Ballard has spoken about the concept of Tower Time in ways that are essential, impactful, and charmingly witty. As a primitivist and farmer, her words ring true in my generation's ears alongside the devastating doomsaying and, conversely, the carefree consumers. This work may be her most important yet, as it not only lovingly crafts things one can actually DO but puts into context the act of ritual through the lens of a deeply personal journey into understanding where we go from here. Here's to the coming flames and the bright flowers that will bloom from the ashes of the old paradigm.
—*Becky Beyer, Blood and Spicebush*

I am fortunate to live in the same community as Byron Ballard. She is a teacher, leader, priestess, gardener who motivates and inspires me by her service to our community. When asked she speaks to our community, in a small people packed room, about Tower Times. Byron listens to our concerns and questions with empathy. She encourages us to reach out and connect to each other, to work together to make our community strong and "resilient." To act fearlessly to protect these ancient mountains that are our home. Byron writes, as she speaks, from her heart. Earth Works is her heart for our community and yours. It is a roadmap for healing yourself, your community, and the piece of earth you call home. Byron's authentic voice offers honest, practical wisdom and guidance woven together with a collection of poetic ceremonies and blessings for creating "circles on the ground." This is a book to read and use now and in the future.
—*Lisa Svencicki, owner Raven and Crone, Asheville*

Earth Works is a shining beacon of hope in a truly turbulent world. Byron Ballard shares an immense amount

of personal wisdom and experience while guiding the reader into establishing a solid spiritual practice rooted in self-reflection, personal awareness, community building, social consciousness, and engagement with the land.
—*Chris Orapello, artist, author, and cohost of Down at the Crossroads*

As grounded as one of her Appalachian Mountains, Byron Ballard gives us an antidote to angst and despair in her newest book, *Earth Works*. Here you will find sensible instructions on building community, on pathfinding a sustainable future, and on personal resilience in a world gone mad. Byron gives us the keys to create powerful rituals, to uncover the sacred in our lives and our homes, to protect ourselves from harm, and to re-enchant our world. By the power of the Goddess and our grannies' apron strings, Byron Ballard's *Earth Works* provides the homely wisdom we need to survive and thrive as we surf the chaos of Tower Time. Let Byron Ballard's *Earth Works* unlock the ancient wisdom we need to survive and thrive as we surf the chaos of Tower Time.
—*Caroline Kenner, Washington Witch doctor*

Byron Ballard has written a book to call us back to ourselves. The greatest threat of Tower Time is that our fear may make us forget our own true names. Tumbling and twisting as we fall headfirst from the lightning-blasted tower, we forget that we know how to fly. Byron's book is a drumbeat, played next to a blazing bonfire, that reminds us who we are and why we are here. This is a book for Tower Time—and for the times to come.
—*Hecate Demeter*

This is a proactive guide during trying times for those of us who are "land tied." Byron outlines for us practical ways to strengthen our ties to hearth and home while also being effective priestesses to our home planet and our family of all life around us.
—*Debra L. Burris, farmer and astrophysicist*

I, as well as you, have been handed an important document. A book for tearing down the old rusting structures that no longer suit, in favor of new, stronger, taller towers of community, resiliency and strength. Let us use the soothing voice and strength of words of the inimitable Byron Ballard to build a new world through this work. These ceremonies will change us all for the better.
—*Amy Blackthorn, Author of Blackthorn's Botanical Magic*

All the wisdom, worry, and care woven thoughtfully into a rich tapestry full of guidance that feels like a master work. Quintessential Byron Ballard, and if anyone is qualified to say so, it's me.
—*Star Bustamonte, Mystic South Conference*

xii

Contents

Foreword

I first met Byron back in early 2000, just a few weeks after I had moved from Maryland to western North Carolina. I'd moved to be near my aging father and was wondering what sort of Pagan community I'd find down here in the Bible Belt. My father already knew about Byron through a theatrical production she had directed in Asheville and had been quick to let me know "there's another witch in town!" Byron and I connected through The Witches' Voice website, and my worries about community were over. Turns out, as I told my dad, there were actually lots of Witches in town. Byron is a community builder who reveres the concept of hospitality, and I soon felt right at home.

Both of us Witches, passionate environmentalists and gardeners, feminists, ritualists, and tarot readers (yes, we're the ones your pastor warned you about), we became friends and met fairly often at Asheville's iconic Earth Fare market for coffee and some conversational cauldron stirring. Our discussions ranged widely but usually returned to the environmental and social issues of our time. Logic and intuition both told us that the Earth was entering a time of crisis and ecological breakdown and that there would be severe accompanying social crises. How we might help mitigate this—save what can be saved, heal what can be healed—was our biggest question.

We got together for one of our coffee klatches a week or so after 9/11, and the discussion quickly turned to our shock and horror—and eventually to what we had both seen so clearly in the repeated, heartrending footage of that disaster—the Tower card of the tarot.

The tarot is much more than a way of divining the future. It offers psychological insights, spiritual guidance, and a way of connecting with the world of spirit. Every card has multiple meanings and also draws meaning from the cards around it in a layout.

Some cards are more equivocal than others. The Tower is unequivocal—sudden, unexpected, destructive change and the crumbling of solid structures, physical or psychological. We realized this card, which shows figures falling from a lightning-struck tower, was perfectly symbolic of what we had been speaking of for so long. That it should be so accurately depicted in reality was not only horrifying, it was a major wake-up call. "It's a card for our times," Byron said. "We're in Tower Time."

And once again, the conversation came around to "What can we do?"

Now, almost sixteen years later, the crumbling of the tower of our unsustainable way of life proceeds apace. I write this foreword in the aftermath of hurricanes Harvey, which decimated Houston, and Irma, which decimated a large swath of the Caribbean, most of Florida, and gave the southern East Coast a kick in the teeth in passing. Both were huge, record-breaking storms. In addition to the many stories of environmental problems, my social media and news feeds are full of accusations of treason, calls for impeachment, the gutting of environmental regulations, pollution run rampant, the threat of nuclear war, Nazis and the Ku Klux Klan marching proudly, faces to the camera.

It's clear that we have many hard and necessary choices to make.

Byron believes, as I do, that these choices must be based in an approach to the natural world that is reverent and prioritizes the ecosystem on which we depend for our very lives over individual rights to pollute, extract, strip-mine, and profit. She knows that this reverent and life-affirming approach requires being open to the voices of the spirit world, of the Ancestors, the land spirits, the consciousness that lies behind the nature that we see. There is an intelligence to nature. We must work with it, not against it, if we are to survive and live well.

Of course, the news is not all bad. There have been tremendous scientific breakthroughs in the past few years—too many to mention here, but I think we can look forward to nonpolluting, nonextractive, renewable electricity, and major breakthroughs in pollution remediation, recycling, and agriculture over the next couple of decades. But the key to rebuilding after the tower has fallen lies in the hearts and minds of those who have the courage and determination to rebuild. If you're reading this book, you're probably one of them.

I doubt the tower of our civilization will fall in one shattering crash. I think, rather, that we will have a series of heartrending and terrifying environmental and humanitarian crises, failures of technology, and confrontations with human nature. We will need to wrestle with fear, stand in our truth, and work hard to create the future we know is possible. In Earth Works, Byron offers us both practical and spiritual solutions to the question of what we can do. She shows us how we can mitigate the destruction, rebuild from the rubble, and create sustainable, supportive community. But more than that, she gives us a way of looking at the world that is animistic and inclusive, respects the web of life, and helps us build a civilization that is a creative part of that web, not its destroyer.

If you want to connect with the earth and help heal the damage we have done to our environment, read this book carefully. Make the ceremonies, practices, and homely, low-tech life hacks part of your daily life. Reach out to others in your area who think as you do and form groups to work with some of those ideas. We live in rapidly changing times, and the future is up for grabs. The book you are holding is both map and manual.

—Diotima Mantineia, Urania's Well

Introduction

This book should be called Earth Works because it has been much like moving mountains to get it written. When I first named the phenomenon of these cultural shifts "Tower Time" sometime late in the Pleistocene Era, my brain kept churning the concept and working with practical solutions, ways we could move from the relative safety of "sustainability" to the more practical place of "resilience."

For several years, when friends and colleagues have asked about my current writing project, I've told them about this book of ceremonies and rituals. I describe it as the "Tower Time" book and lament that it has taken so long to manifest. But the truth of the matter is that the concept of Tower Time has moved me to a near frenzy of community building and speaking and working, and the writing of it has been slow in coming.

I've often written of the little Wednesday evening group that we called "the Alewives Sisterhood of the Sacred Soil" and the impact that group had on my life and work. It has mostly disbanded now, but many of us still meet occasionally and maintain a close sisterhood. My dreams of reviving it may come true—now that I have at last finished the Tower Time book. In that group, we mulled over schemes and hatched plots. We wept and laughed and cursed the patriarchy. In that group, the idea of Tower Time was fleshed out and made whole.

The concept has moved from my writing and speaking to other mouths and other minds. Other Pagan writers (notably bloggers John Beckett and Hecate Demeter's Daughter) sometimes write about the cultural shiftings under this rubric, and mostly they credit me, for which I am grateful. At a recent American Academy of Religion conference, the Contemporary Pagan Studies Group created a panel called "Magic in the Time of the Tower." Blogger Chas Clifton suggested the following in his blog post "Tower Time Is Not as Simple as You Think."

> You might fix it first by being responsible for as much of your own life as you can. I don't mean that you have to weave your own cloth. Just don't be the person who can't change a tire, sew on a button, or understand a loan document.
>
> And find your community. Not merely the online community: Is your Instagram follower going to bring supper over when you're sick? Can you call your Facebook friend if you need a ride to the doctor?
>
> Not just a religious community either. When my Jeep drove itself into a gully near the house, I did not look for a Pagan friend but rather a neighbor with a big winch-equipped truck who likes solving mechanical problems. Depending on your neighbors means you cannot just condemn them for their voting patterns and otherwise ignore them. But that only works if the neighbor can depend on you. If it really is "Tower Time," the response is to work at the ground level.
>
> —Notes from Hardscrabble Creek blog
> (http://blog.chasclifton.com/)

We are in this now, for better or for worse. When I am approached and asked about timelines, I am not very helpful. But when I am approached about what can be done to mitigate some of the sharpness and calamity, I am more forthcoming. I speak of circles on the ground, of making everything local, of gathering in colleagues and allies and sometimes finding them in unexpected places.

So this then is "the Tower Time book." It is not the first word on the subject, nor will it be the last. I certainly hope it will not because this cultural shift will wriggle and adapt its techniques, which will require us all to stay on our toes and adjust our protocols and tools accordingly. Earth Works is a patchwork of existing writings on the subject, plus all my latest thoughts about where we are. It includes some lamentations about how slowly we are moving and also some glory hallelujahs about how far we've come.

There have been moments of revelation, mostly while sitting around a fire with snacks and drinks. A sequence emerged of lighting signal fires (inspired by the *Lord of the Rings* films), saving the scrolls (a dream of the great and lost library at Alexandria), and leaping onto a way that has been made clear (following the destruction of the Roman temple at Palmyra). Some of that is reflected here, but much of it is still revealing itself. And some of it is for you to hear and proclaim because Tower Time does not belong to me. I have only named a thing that I have observed and felt compelled to act upon. For the rest, it will be down to history to speak of what we did or didn't do. With any luck, there will be a song or two, and a poem.

When I started writing about folk magic, my motto was "attitude is everything"—an idea I apply to my magical practice and to my life. We can approach this change that many of us feel by cowering in fear, or we can pluck up our courage and creativity and meet our fate head-on.

I hope these long-awaited pages afford you some ideas for your own circles on the ground. Or that they encourage you when the way seems too rocky and hard.

Thank you for reading it, and good luck to you and yours in the going forward.

—H. Byron Ballard, March 2018

CHAPTER ONE

GOING TO GROUND

LOVE IN THE TIME of TOWERS

I don't remember precisely when it began, this quiet knowing that has grown—for me—into a certainty. It began with a pinch of insight, a glint of what was happening globally, reflected in local events. It was more than a lack of harmony, of simple chaotic modern life. This feeling hinted at larger activity, a shift in the zeitgeist, a disturbance in the force.

At Sacred Space Conference 2017, I arrived within a half hour of the first talk I was scheduled to give. "The People's Craft—Folk Magic and Its Peasant Roots" was supposed to be a rousing exploration of some of the commonalities of folk magic across different cultures and the fascination with those practices among modern Pagans.

It turned into a sermon focused on resilience and the power of revolution. It became a plea for Pagans to see clearly what must be done for our biosphere and our species. Pacing the large room (wearing the same battered jeans that I'd traveled in for nine hours from North Carolina), I preached as my Methodist forebears did. I invited the attendees to consider peasant life. I brandished a pitchfork.

Tower Time. It has become my mantra as well as an ongoing vision and occasional nightmare. It has been in front of me for a decade or more since the day I sat on a friend's sunny porch, drinking wine and comparing our visions. That seems like a faraway dream now, a kinder time, a time less fraught and more hopeful.

In brief, I have come to know through unverifiable personal gnosis (UPG)—dreams, visions, ponderings, discussions with colleagues—that we are living in the times when the top-down and toxic systems that some of us call patriarchy are in the process of collapse. Because I am a lifelong tarot reader, the image that returns to my mind again and again is the Tower, sweet number sixteen.

The clear knowing that I have felt has grown more insistent in the intervening years. It is this: we are living in times when these massive, ancient, and toxic systems that have both created civilization as we know it and doomed it are crashing under their own weight of history and grief. It is the death throes of patriarchy that we are experiencing, and it will die as it has lived—in violence and oppression and injustice and death.

Madness. Friends and coreligionists opine that I have been seduced by cyclical end-of-days hysteria, that I am guilty of buying into the ever-increasing wall of apocalypse noise from conservative Christians. Or that I am cleverly fearmongering for control of my social media followers.

I've heard it all. But I've also heard concurring murmurings from colleagues as far afield as New Zealand. This feeling—this strange knowing—is visiting others of my kind. We are, as the Cheshire cat purred, all mad here.

It is concerning, confusing, and rather exciting.

Fast-forward to the recent unpleasantness of the 2016 election cycle and the subsequent fear and lethargy that have beset so many of my friends and colleagues, my congregation, my neighbors. Interfaith groups gather in ragged circles, loathing the news, weeping for the future. Social media is rife with hand-wringing and angst. Systems failing. Toppling institutions grappling with their own demises, recalibrating as they fall, as they morph into new systems, ones that serve different masters.

The visions of Tower Time have never been solely about the collapse, which I want to stress early on and return to throughout the first part of this book. This is not a gloom-and-doom scenario. I invite you to explore the next steps, the best step. As the Tower falls, it is incumbent on all of us who can act, to create what I have been calling "circles on the ground"—active and well-thought-out alternatives to what we've come to know. Alternatives that work where you are, that include everyone, that take planet and people into consideration. We have been trained to abhor vacuums, we humans. And power vacuums most of all. The easiest thing to do is to insert a new kind of savior, the perfect strongman to see us through. It's a very old pattern—a pattern I'd like to see broken once and for all. Hierarchy is such an efficient system and easily reinstalled. It will take foresight and planning to not reinstate the very systems we want to change. We will have to look beyond jargon and comforting platitudes—the newspeak that has become a permanent part of every news cycle, at every news outlet. And it will take weaving new connections and possibly redefining who and what our tribe is. That is uncomfortable work—the sort of work that leads us to consider our own personal ethics and priorities as well as our own mortality and limitations.

These circles are about permaculture and relearning old skills and being ready to step into any systems vacuum that occurs and to step in with an easily understandable, navigable, and workable set of protocols that we know to be effective because we are already doing them. They are in place in our communities, modeling in microcosm what can happen on a larger field. It is about relocalizing our needs and globalizing our information base while we can. We can begin by asking questions. Where does our food come from? What are our water sources? Are either of those protected in any reasonable way? Who are our neighbors? Who are our coreligionists? Where do our interdependencies lie?

But we have to do this now. In fact, we should have done it several years ago. The good news is that some people have. Check out what's happening with food sourcing in Detroit. Google the possibilities for energy sources, many available in your area.

I am part of a Wednesday evening garden-and-all-sorts group called the Alewives. When we first gathered several years ago, our resident gardening expert spoke of lighting signal fires to show other small circles that there was possibility in the ingathering of both people and resources. We imagined those signal fires leaping up on the ridges around us, bringing news from hilltop to hilltop in the old and mythic ways that we mostly know from the *Lord of the Rings* films.

I have found that most people ignore signal fires. In fact, Cassandra and her woes became a sort of strange comfort as I kept sounding the same note of opportunity amidst decay. Again and again and again. And then Trump happened. Bannon happened. Viewing the events of the past year as catalytic is a helpful way of leaning in to the possibilities and opportunities of these times that are our times.

The election and its aftermath have changed some things, acted as a signal fire of sorts. The group at that first evening at Sacred Space nodded in agreement.

Throughout the conference, colleagues who had attended that frenzied talk told me of their work in their communities to create those circles on the ground. But the price of this visioning, this anxiety, this unmitigated fury is high, and it includes burnout, illness, confusion. So easy for these times to overtake us, for our dreams to become revolving nightmares as the needs outweigh the energy and attention necessary to address them.

A few years ago (on the edge of burnout myself and grasping at notions of self-care), I developed a Pick Three philosophy—I chose the three areas about which I was most passionate and focused on them, clinging like a limpet. It doesn't mean all the other justice issues don't touch me or concern me. It means I will be actively working on those three.

I encourage you to consider your own choice—especially if you are in danger of shutting down because you are overwhelmed. I know there are good people working on so many important causes. I stand as an ally, even if I am not in the trenches, on many of those issues. Because I can't support all of them effectively. None of us can.

If you are overwhelmed with a desire to help, look at your community and see if there are people who are hungry—because they are there. Look to see if there is land that needs protection—because there is. You can help. You can feel. It's okay to do both. Think of your friends and colleagues who have been triggered by recent events—check in with them. Check in with the people who are always strong but now are quiet. Send them your good love and attention.

CRED

I am convinced that the current resident of the Oval Office—along with his colleagues in dismantling the republic—is the catalyst this work has been waiting for. During the campaign, as more and more people likened him to Hitler, I couldn't help thinking he was this republic's Caligula. As we consider the recalibrations of these failing systems and we consider how far down the bottom lies that the republic must hit, we will also be treated to scenes from Bizarro World. Stripping national parks of their resources, the ongoing (and increasingly peculiar) saga of repealing the Affordable Care Act, the defunding of Meals on Wheels—each focus stranger than the one before—these are symptoms of the shifting of systems, much as Caligula made his horse a senator or forced men with better hair than his to shave it off. The nonsensical world we inhabit seems strange because it is strange.

It is important for Earth-loving folks and Earth religionists to resist the temptation to cower in fear of this strangeness, this meanness. Now is the time to practice all that we preach about interconnectedness and the divinity of the biosphere. Do we love it (and each other) enough to fight? Enough to focus our considerable will and intentions on the survival of our species?

This is our time, the times we were made for. Ground. Center. Focus. The signal fires have been lit, and we have much work to do to make the world we want for our kith and kindred. And let us consider the Earth—and all she holds—our kith, our kindred.

We are shaky now, frightened, angry. If you are a theist of some sort, go to your altar and renew your daily spiritual practice. Go outside. Remember. Remember who you are and where you are and your golden wild heart. Find your tribe and sit in circle with other tribes, either literal or virtual.

CR℘℘

In trying to understand this intuition and what it all means, I periodically trot out the Tower Time document file (see Addenda) and post it to social media. There are new readers certainly, but there are also readers who return to it and find new meaning. As the file grows, of course, there are different ideas or invitations or evaluations.

Much of what I think about and write about is by way of motivating the people who read or hear my words. But I also like to be a purveyor of a little comfort and joy when I can. In spite of the Fear not! Fear not! palaver, people are afraid. I'm afraid. If this shifting is as big as I (and so many others) think and the end of it is so far down the cultural road that we'll never see it, and if we have nuclear power and weaponry and power-besotted dictators and no real authority over the people who lead us, that can make for a very emotionally shaky life.

I take most of my cues from nature, as do many of you. When I am faced with a difficult problem, I attack it from many sides, but I ultimately end up asking myself how it's dealt with in the natural world. And as I position myself to dispense some comfort and joy, I naturally look for remedies in the green and mountainous lands around me.

Relating these cultural shifts to the workings of the natural world was important early on in this exploration as I relayed in the following essay.

Going to Ground in Tower Time

Early in the Gulf of Mexico oil well disaster, the Deepwater Horizon explosion in 2010—when it was apparent that the problem would not be solved quickly—a small group of women gathered in our small Goddess temple. They brought rum and watermelon, and the room soon filled with clouds of rich incense. Chants for Yemaya began softly; rattles were gently rattled. As the spirit of despair was tamped down and the strands of joy and connection wove themselves into the singing and the smoke, the chants grew stronger. The dancing, which was little more than rhythmic stomping, began. Our community's Beloved Crone seemed to be speaking an unknown language, as water bottles were chugged and offerings were made to Ancestors and Deities. The woman nearest the altar—the one who had issued the invitation—muttered prayers and knelt on the floor, singing the holy names. As she had promised, she flung herself full-length in front of the wooden altar and begged the sea Goddesses for mercy. The singing and chanting continued for some time until the participants were dry and tired, eyes streaming tears of grief and too much smoke.

Sometimes when we pray, we forget that prayer is not simply sending our best intention into the universe. For those of us who see the Ancestral Goddesses as incorporeal beings who have some authority and ability in the world, the prayers and the singing honor beloved ones who are near us but are not us. The invocations in which we implore them to fix our lives or clean up our messes or show us a way through are requests and bargainings. We understand that we have a part in the relationship, but we do not have control. We are not the boss. We are participants in an ancient cycle of creation and destruction and re-creation.

And sometimes the answer is no. Sometimes the answer is you got yourself into this and you and your people are going to have to fix what you broke, you are going to have to take personal responsibility and get yourselves out of it.

Our community was far away from the horror and ineptitude that was the Gulf disaster, high in the southern mountains. But we are none of us "away," are we? We are all connected—physically, spiritually, and electronically. We know that today's oil slick is picked up by next month's hurricane and deposited in our organic gardens on our longed-for heirloom tomatoes.

We work ourselves into a frenzy of grief and guilt and spiritual activity. We open ourselves to the sorrow and anger and filter it as best we can. We meet for coffee and walks, and we talk for hours on the phone. Gentling the community in its outrage, cushioning it from outright despair. We are blown about by the winds and waves of all that assails us, and sometimes the only place to go for succor, for comfort, is away from the computer and the phone and the endless cups of coffee. To the garden, to the woods, to the earth.

There's an evocative expression that has become a keystone for my work in the community of late. The phrase "going to ground" has taken on new significance as we stand in this challenging Tower Time. To "go to ground" is to run pell-mell back to the den or burrow, to find someplace safe to hide. To make a run for it. Foxes do it. Rabbits do it.

Since the earthquakes that ripped through Haiti in January of 2010, there has been a series of human-made and natural disasters that have been unremitting in their intensity, and we have been subsumed in the wake of them.

How many times have I forgotten—forgotten!—the people of Nashville, TN, who were inundated with the rising waters of the Cumberland. The seaquake and tsunami and the ongoing nuclear tragedy in Japan sets on already-heavy hearts. There have been storms and volcanoes, floods and bombers. One after another, a laundry list of devastation that can barely be acknowledged, much less comprehended.

In my community work, in my social networking, in counseling seekers with Mother Grove congregants, I have been calling the times in which we move Tower Time. I imagine that the vast foundations are cracking and we are in the top of the Tower, where we must leap outward or be crushed with the weight of this six-thousand-year-old system in its death throes.

Tower Time—we must engage or perish. We cannot remain untouched, uninvolved, because it does involve us. All of us. But the overwhelming-ness of it—how do we find the wings to fly from the Tower? How do we glide away from the mess and the pain and not look back to those falling faster and faster?

We don't. We can't. It is not in our nature. And so we bear the wounds and we keep on, even as we feel the spiritual lifeblood leaking out, only to be replaced by ennui and despair. In our circles, we call for "grounding." We speak the words of guided meditations in which roots grow from our feet and sink, gratefully, into the earth.

Grounding. Going to ground.

We are furry mammals, warm animals, wounded animals. We have tried to think ourselves out of this mess. We've tried to ritualize ourselves out of this mess. But you know what a wounded animal does. A rabbit or groundhog or badger? They go to ground and lick their wounds. They hide in their burrow, in the very womb of the earth, and they take time to heal and regroup.

I'm not suggesting we bury our heads in the sand, that we run away from our spiritual responsibilities. I'm advising that when the going gets too much for you to bear, you remember that you are a warm animal and you have a special option because of that. You can go to your burrow to recuperate and lick your wounds. Then you can return to your community renewed as the clever and powerful badger that you are.

Finally, here's my advice to a friend (and to all of you) who was feeling ungrounded, displaced, abandoned by Goddess and community. I offer it here for you, with a few additions and points of clarification, if you have need of it. Here is a too-brief checklist of possibilities, if you are finding yourself in the midst of the falling Tower, unable to do more than gasp as the earth rises to meet you.

Throughout the chapters of this book, you will find ways to achieve the following:

Set an energy trap.

Set wards; set your energetic shields. If you can't do that, let your community know, and they will shield you until you can.

Renew your home altar.

Go out to your land and ask for help. Invoke your Ancestors and the land spirits. Take an offering. Bring some of the dirt in with you. Put it in your pockets, on your altar.

Put brick dust at the secondary entrances to the house—windows, back door, crawl space door. Not a line, just a drop.

Put white dust at the front door—this can be baking soda, stone ground flour, salt.

Light a rue candle if you have one.

Spend time outside, sitting on the dear old earth.

Invite others to join you in a simple ritual of healing and grounding.

The best advice I have is "go to ground." Earth everywhere. Dirt in your pockets, dirt in your shoes.

Grounded, with shields up and wards in place, breathe deeply and evaluate where you are.

Go to ground, sisters and brothers. Earth everywhere. It's Tower Time.

You may choose to go to ground anytime that feels right to you. What we are doing as interlocking communities and villages and as a species is daunting and at times overwhelming. Find whatever space you need to renew your energy and determination, to rest your body and your mind and your ragged spirit.

That's why I've written this book. It is laid out in easy-to-use chapters that begin with a long essay about the particular subject, and some finish with a complete ritual that you can do with your family or coreligionists to prepare yourselves for the changes that we are beginning to experience right now. The final part of the book gives you some examples of larger celebrations that you may choose to do within your wider community. These are templates and tools; they are not holy writ. I invite and indeed encourage you to change them in whatever feels best for your surroundings, your experience, and your temperament.

And so it begins.

CHAPTER TWO

IN THE BOUGHS OF TREES

Rock-a-bye, baby,
In the treetop.
When the wind blows, the cradle will rock.
When the bough breaks, the cradle will fall,
And down will come baby, cradle and all.
—traditional

AN INVITATION TO EARTH HONORING

Like the admonition not to carry all one's eggs in a single basket, this nursery rhyme is poignant in this time of change and wonder and despair. I am sitting here at the keyboard, occasionally checking the news and taking emails and calls from people who feel they are at the end of their rope, both economically and spiritually. I'm doing a wedding this weekend, and that usually requires several meetings and phone calls with the couple as they iron out the ceremony they expect to never repeat. But the soon-to-be couple is mostly silent, dealing with a crashing economy, a sickness that could at any moment become catastrophic, and the death of a family pet. They can hardly think about their Big Day because life has come close to flattening them.

What is going on? Is it—as we sometimes read on church signs in the South—the end of the world? Or is it only (only!) the end of the world as we know it right now? We devour explanations by astrologers; we read books and blogs about permaculture and sustainability. We are growing victory gardens, unsure if victory can even be defined.

This is certainly the end of cheap petroleum and all that resource allowed us to do and be. It won't be cheaper to get lettuce and potentially perilous spinach shipped in fresh from California to the East Coast. As more and more of our prime arable land is given over to strip shopping centers and trophy homes, we find that local droughts aren't the only reason we can't locate hay to feed our livestock. The news cycle sometimes brings us stories of the impending doom of Colony Collapse Disorder in our apian neighbors, but that doesn't seem to sink in on a local level.

Where do you get your food? Is the soil safe to grow in even if it isn't covered with concrete? As we get to know our local resources—gasp!—even meet our neighbors, we will find that everything we truly need is close at hand. Farmer vendors bring fat bushels of fresh produce to tailgate markets throughout the country, and Americans are relearning how to shop in markets and talk to the people who actually grow the food we are eating. Slowly we are learning to live more lightly on the planet and to know that resources—even in the US—are finite and that we shouldn't and—now can't—use more than we need.

With the end of cheap petroleum, we may also see the end of the hyperconsumerism that has driven our economy for decades. Americans have the opportunity to beat this learning curve and to come through the current set of crises with a set of usable skills, some sharpened tools in our tool belts for living. Even if it only means canning tomatoes, making your own cider, and growing some of your own food as most of our grandparents did. New knowledge about sustainable agriculture gives us improved ways to do what people have been doing since the very beginning—taking care of ourselves, our families, and each other. It is not such a bad way to live, but it is very different from much of our American culture here at the dawn of this new era. We are learning and relearning and sharing information on the how-tos and the why-fors that have become necessary again.

For many, this is also a time of spiritual crisis. Earth religions and New Age philosophies are seeing a great influx of seekers, and the gentle discipline of Buddhism has made inroads with Westerners both here and in Europe. But we are also seeing Earth religionists who view what is happening to the planet, have read the popular books about using "abundance mentality" to heal and to survive the financial crises and can't seem to manifest what they want in their lives. If they are Pagan peoples who have a pantheon of deities that are the hub of their worship experience, they may be pondering the age-old question of how a benevolent and immanent deity can allow hundreds of pilgrims to be trampled at the Ka'aba or killed while visiting a temple in India during Durga Puja.

They may have left the Abrahamic religions they practiced as children and have chosen a more Earth-centered path that seems natural, following the cycle of the agricultural year. They have chosen religions of flower crowns and baby blessings and yet... and yet... how to explain the sudden death of a child? The terminal illness of a young mother? Mountaintop removal? Poison in the drinking water of the most vulnerable people on the planet?

As a priestess and ritualist, I work to give these inexplicable and life-altering events some meaning for the people going through them. As we face these worldwide crises, I know we can find ways to get through them together, to forge stronger and healthier communities, to deepen both our spiritual practices and our commitment to them.

I am an occasional writer for several printed and online magazines, and I find that the responses I get through cyberspace are filled with a yearning to know more, which is only human. But there is also a sense that people want to do more. We are so good at reading up on something, studying, filling our heads with facts and information. There is a hunger for a relationship with the land on which we live and an equally deep need to do more than simply read about it. People want to explore the Earth through the lens of ceremony and spirit. They want to learn the ways of the planet—weather, water, soil.

There is a sense of the rightness of making rituals out of this deep experience in nature, and many people don't have resources to do that kind of creative work. They are stretching their notion of what is and isn't religion to fit the needs and movement of the planet.

We're going to start with some definition of terms and with the basics of crafting a ritual.

I was invited to hang out with some very nice people recently—the folks who stage celebrations of the solstices and equinoxes in a local botanical garden. They had been creating those rites in an organic and intuitive way—taking stock of who was available and what that person's skill sets were. But they found themselves at a loss when it came time to organize the event. What goes where? Our initial meeting saw dozens of long white sheets decorating the walls of the gazebo, sheets with scribbled remarks and diagrams of where to go and when. It was a joy to talk about the parts of ritual and to help them give some shape to an upcoming celebration. In that pleasant gazebo at a university botanical garden, we wrestled with what makes a ritual work for the participants and for the creators.

We began by defining some of the words that have become commonplace and have, therefore, lost some of their original intent and meaning. It's an excellent place for us to begin too. Establishing a common and agreed-upon lexicon gives us the opportunity to communicate clearly and eliminate some of the confusion about what each of the participants is agreeing to present.

What is a ritual? A ceremony? A celebration? Let's create some working definitions of these events and find out how interchangeable they are.

A *ritual* is a vessel in which celebrants and seekers perform a series of intentional words, movement, or sound to create a desired outcome. It generally has religious or spiritual overtones and may include worship, words of praise, a ceremonial sharing of food and drink (cakes and ale).

A *ceremony* is a self-contained piece within a larger ritual. I also use this term to mean a smaller or more personal ritual.

Celebration should be self-explanatory and is not spiritual so much as spirited. It's an organized way to come together in community around a specific set of circumstances. It can include all the elements in the other forms but may not include anything but bottles of bubbles for blowing and a couple of drums. A loosely structured joyful event.

You may know that I hold a Master of Fine Arts degree, the terminal degree in my field, which is theatre. My training (for many years) was in the workings of theatre—I have been a playwright, an actor, a director, a designer. So I bring a sense of that to religious ceremonies, I think. But not too much, because I resent when religion tries to be theatre. For many years, I also celebrated with a coven of people who were mostly actors, and our rituals tended to be simple and heartfelt but not terribly drama-filled. Possibly because we did theatre as well and knew some of the differences between one and the other.

But there are many similarities too. Theatre and religion come from a central source in the West, and even today the places where drama and ritual are made are strikingly similar. There's a place for spectators, a place for participants, a place to dress, an area where the focus is drawn. And the elements of both are similar—the gathering in of spectators, the preparation of the celebrants, the energy exchange between the observer and the observed. There's a sensitivity to energy and flow that is important to each and a striving to keep the pace moving and the spectators engaged.

When I left grad school, I told myself I would return to school at some undetermined future time and study for a doctorate in theatre history since I could not advance any further academically with theatre practice (at least at that time). There was a particular event and era I dreamed of researching: the reemergence of theatre into western Europe through the mechanism of the *quem quaeritis* trope.

Imagine that the church has basically banned theatre as a sinful, paganish pastime, frivolous and ungodly. (For those of you who know the origins of classical theatre in the religious observances of ancient Hellas, you may laugh bitterly about the "ungodly" part.) Liturgy and angelic music are acceptable, however. Hold that thought.

The annual observance of the Resurrection at Easter requires a certain amount of drama so that the unlettered folk will understand the significance of that long-ago event upon their short and dull lives. With a choir on either side of the dark nave, there grew a kind of call and response between them that told the story of the Marys arriving at the tomb only to find the stone rolled away and the beloved body gone. Led by our girl Mary Magdalene—the only one of the master's followers who wasn't lying on a couch somewhere weeping and wailing—the women had come to do what women always do: tidy up. They came to make sure the body was neatly wrapped, anointed with sweet oils, and laid out in a respectful way.

An angel stood in the open doorway and asked, Whom do you seek? And was answered by one or all of the women—Jesus of Nazareth, who was crucified. The women were informed that he had risen from the dead and they were to go throughout the land, proclaiming the Good News.

It's almost like a telenovela, isn't it? Especially if you know the sexy backstory of the Magdalene and the dear departed dead.

There are several theories about how this heightened bit of liturgy, this lightly dramatized trope, brought theatre back from its hiatus, but for our purposes we'll imagine that some tenors or boy sopranos in the choir got dressed up in long robes and wigs to make it all more visual for the peasantry and that one beautiful Easter morning, they all went out on the porch of the church and acted out the encounter with the angel, who was probably played by a Very Important Man of the town.

Theatre returned, at last, to Europe, and from this simple trope grew the extraordinary treasure trove of mystery and miracle plays that in turn fueled the English theatre renaissance. You know, Marlowe, Jonson, Henslow, Brome, and that precocious lad, Will Shakespeare.

You've been ever so patient.

This story is to illustrate that theatre grew from the womb of liturgy in those less-than-dark ages. In fact, theatre and religion are inextricably bound together and have been from the earliest times. The sympathetic magic of wandering hunter-gatherers was a theatre of necessity, a theatre of magic, a ritual of survival. The sacred festivals of ancient Hellas left to us compelling dramas that are performed to this very day, first staged as tribute to divinities whose names people Western history.

So when I—actor, director, playwright—sit down to create a public ritual for Mother Grove Goddess Temple, I bring to that task all those years of training and experience. But my roots are still in those stony grounds, in the perfect acoustics of Epidaurus and Delphi, in theatre dedicated to Dionysus that brings the Divines within arm's reach of those who adore them.

The late and terribly wise Terry Pratchett wrote of the importance of "boffo" in the successful practice of witchcraft. Boffo is a bit of swagger and drama that reassures the client that magic is actually taking place. Public ritual requires a bit of boffo too and the addition of creativity as well as a deep knowledge of the holy day to be celebrated. But if you start with a basic template for ritual, you can build on that and still have a solid core of ceremony that will help those attending to feel part of a community, as well as giving them the chance to participate in a religious practice that harkens back to the origins of religion in the West.

In addition to public rituals on each of the holy days on the Wheel of the Year, I work to give inexplicable and life-altering events some meaning for the people going through them. As we face these worldwide crises, I know we can find ways to get through them together, to forge stronger and healthier communities, to deepen both our spiritual practices and our commitment to them.

There is a sense of the rightness and comfort in making rituals out of our deep experiences with the changing seasons, but many people don't have resources for that kind of creative work. They are stretching their notion of what is and isn't religion to fit the needs and movement of the planet. But my email often contains requests for ways to mark those things ceremonially.

What are the parts of a ritual? After many years of creating ritual on my own, in groups and as a priestess working with congregants and interested seekers, I have come to have a sense of what basic pieces make up the structural building blocks of an effective ritual. Some of the parts can be greatly enhanced through ritual drama and congregational participation, and depending on the kind of ritual, some parts may be omitted entirely. But using this template can help you create a complete and satisfying ceremony.

My template looks like this:
- Preparation for ritual through purification (smudge, bath, anointing)
- Ingathering (if it is more than a handful of people
- Welcome and housekeeping (the bathrooms are there; turn off your damned phones)
- Calling in of elements/directions, ancestors/deities, and/or creation of intentional/sacred space
- Invocation
- Setting the intention
- Meditation or other preparation
- Instruction in technique, if required
- Raising energy through movement or sound (chant, singing, toning, dance, drumming)
- Releasing the energy
- Grounding through sharing of food and drink
- Thanking and releasing elements/directions/ancestors/deities

- Devocation
- Benediction

I have found this order to work for most types of rituals, but it is not engraved in stone. Ritual, like good theatre, must be a living thing, a creature brought into existence for specific purposes. You will also know that this is merely an outline. Once the Divines are invited in and welcomed (or more especially if They are not), this creature that is ritual is no longer entirely in the hands of those who called. A certain amount of good temper and flexibility will yield the most powerful and delicious part of ritual—the presence of Mystery.

Many religions see the need to mark the transition between the everyday world and the time in which ritual occurs. There is a sense of leaving your baggage behind as you approach deity and move in intentional or sacred space. This transition is sometimes marked with a ritual or literal purification. First Nations' sweat lodges and the Jewish mikvah are some examples of literal purifications that are also symbolic and preparatory.

In many modern circles, the purification is a stylized one and is achieved by wafting smoke onto the participants as they enter the ceremonial circle. White sage has been borrowed from the ceremonies of tribal American Indians, but other herbs useful for ritual purification include cedar, juniper, lavender, and sweetgrass.

Incense is also used. The Catholic, Orthodox, and Anglican congregations are well familiar with the "smells and bells" of some of the more important holy days.

After the ritual purification has taken place, there's a moment where the celebrant helps the participant step across the threshold into the intentional space. This can be done with a light anointing on the forehead with a sweet oil or with pure water. Some women's circles prefer to place a rough spot of ocher onto the center of the participant's forehead. No matter the material used, anointing activates the portal between the worlds and facilitates this transition.

Whether you are celebrating a major holy day with a thousand of your closest friends or a simple ceremony with a small group, it is wise to give yourself some time for the ingathering. This is the place where the purified and anointed participants arrive into the intentional space and take a moment to acknowledge the community that has joined together in this particular time and place. It is an invitation to be part of ritual and to quell the chatter, to circle up.

The celebrants or facilitators should always welcome the participants and do a bit of light housekeeping. Introduce themselves, if the ritual is a public one with different attendees at different times. Be clear about the location of the restrooms, encourage people to turn off mobile phones, review the ritual if that feels necessary. It is by way of welcome, of offering hospitality.

Mark Out the Space or Raising the Circle

It's helpful to set the spatial boundaries that will contain the ritual. You may honor the cardinal directions or the classical elements, spinning an enclosed energy field in which to work. There are dozens of ways and many shapes to play around with. Many modern Pagans are accustomed to a circle, but it isn't the only shape a ceremony can take.

Invoking the Divine/s

If you and your group are theists, you may choose to "call the center," bring in particular allies for the working or honoring particular deities of the season or holy day.

Setting the Intention

Through a consensus process or autonomy by celebrant, set the intention for your ritual. This keeps the participants focused and engaged. You can also accomplish this through group or individual meditation.

Instruction in Technique to Be Used, if Required

Will there be dancing? Chanting? Take a few moments before this part of your ritual to teach the dance or the chant or advise people on the best breathing technique for chanting.

Raising Energy

Sometimes the intention includes the group raising energy and using it in service of the intention. Energy is raised in a number of ways—chant, dance, movement, song, drumming, rattles, handclapping—and all are effective ways to work in a group.

Releasing Energy

We talk in terms of releasing a "cone of power" to send the raised energy to the place we intend to affect. There are several ways to do this.

Grounding

Following the release of energy, it is good to have the group touch the ground or floor in order to earth or ground extra energy. Other grounding techniques that I have used include the ceremony of "cakes and ale," story time, holding each other's hands.

Releasing the Quarters/Opening the Circle

Opening the circle and honoring the work as well as the workers. The words usually parallel the words used to establish the intentional ritual space at the beginning of the rite.

Thanking the Divine/s and Ancestors; Devocation

A sincere expression of thanks for the presence of all the unseen folk who attended your ritual, from Divines to Ancestors to land spirits.

Benediction

These are the final words of blessing. The word comes from the Latin and means "good words." I think of it as "words for going" and a chance to wish the participants a safe home-going.

CR℘

Where can a ritual take place? Anywhere at all. Outdoor public rituals will require the planners to find out what sorts of permits and permissions are required. Security may be a smart idea. And assembling a team of volunteers is a must. Consider parking and carpooling. Don't try to do it alone. It will break you.

You may choose to be outside on private land, and that will require working with the landowner to make sure the space is adequate, checking on insurance specifications, making sure there are bathroom facilities. And put up signs to direct the participants.

You may find available space for occasional rituals that will be loaned to you or can be rented. You may need to sign a use agreement and abide by the rules of the room.

If you have land and a big house, you can choose to create a ritual room, a dedicated space in which to work. That may require you to keep the number of participants low, but you will be safe from prying eyes and public scolds.

What should be worn for ritual? Anything at all and nothing at all. It may depend on the weather and your spiritual tradition and where the event takes place. Some people have dedicated garments—ritual robes, for instance. Street clothes are fine. Sometimes the ritual has a dramatic component and costumes are worn. And Pagans are somewhat notorious for dancing naked in the forest, which is usually called "sky clad." In my experience, not many of us do that with any regularity. Sorry to disappoint you.

Ritualizing events, rites of passage, and the cycles of the natural world is one way to gain clarity as we face drastic Earth changes, as well as the personal changes within our communities. These techniques will give you a refuge when things are scary and a place of strength when things get tough.

Some of us are worried, some of us are terrified, some of us are curiously elated at the prospect that these faulty and stultifying systems are at last crumbling. The hand-wringing over global climate change (with its shadow self—those talk radio folk who pooh-pooh the very notion that humans could have any real effect on a global scale) leads inevitably to a low-level, near-constant terror that somehow we haven't done enough, that we are powerless in a situation that spells our very doom.

Always looking to the power and comfort of nature, I created a ritual that has continued to be both grounding and focusing in the intervening years. It is a ritual honoring trees, our oldest living kindred. The event that precipitated this ritual was the harvesting of several old and revered trees in our community. We chose to create a ritual to honor the loss and the lives of those great trees. We did this ritual in conjunction with the Unitarian Universalist Congregation of the Swannanoa Valley, where it was first enacted.

Ritual Honoring the Trees

We began by creating a circle cast that was all about trees.

North: We welcome the spirit of the great trees of the woodland—the oak and elm and redwood. We remember that they and their offspring are in our houses and in our fireplaces, giving us warmth and shelter in the deep midwinter. Oak and elm and redwood, be with us tonight in the darkness.

East: We welcome the spirit of seeds that sail on the wind—sycamore and ash and mimosa. We also honor those trees that grant us the power of deep communication through their transformation into paper, in book and newspaper and letter from home. Sycamore and ash and mimosa, be with us tonight in the darkness.

South: We welcome the fire of autumn changes, when the maple becomes yellow, red, and orange flames of light as the year darkens. We also honor those trees that succumb to wildfire in the dryness of the seasons so that others may have room to thrive and grow upward. Maple of many colors, be with us tonight in the darkness.

West: We welcome the spirit of the great trees who stand in and by the waters—the cypress, the willow, the birch. They show us ability to withstand change, to flourish in wind and rain. Cypress and willow and birch, be with us tonight in the darkness.

Our circle is cast. We stand in the most sacred of groves, and the oldest of our living kindred are here with us. And so it is.

Then we had a time given over to some teaching and preaching about the importance of trees.

Our long history as humans has been full of trees as symbols. From ancient Sumer, to China, to Africa, to the Druids and Johnny Appleseed and Paul Bunyan, our western history has looked to our still kindred as spiritual and literal shelter, as source of food and shade and revenue. I shake my head when I hear the arguments about the Temple Mound in Jerusalem. Is it a Muslim holy site or a Jewish one? It began, according to the Old Testament, as a grove sacred to the Goddess Asherah. Solomon had it cut down and established a temple on the site of the grove, replacing the trees with a temple built from... you guessed it... trees.

The fabled Cedars of Lebanon. Those great swaths of cedar were used by the ancient Phoenicians for building ships, houses, and temples. The Egyptians used its resin for mummification, and its sawdust was found in pharaohs' tombs. The Epic of Gilgamesh designated the cedar groves of Lebanon as the dwelling place of the gods. Hebrew priests were ordered by Moses to use the bark of the Lebanon cedar in circumcision and the treatment of leprosy. Mature trees are mostly rare now, but there is a vibrant reforestation program throughout Lebanon, and the tree is still used as a symbol on the Lebanese flag.

We moved then into a guided meditation for those in attendance. They were asked to take a deep breath and relax into their seats. Here it is.

Meditation

Close your eyes now and think about those things and people that really nurture you and also nourish you. Be specific—whether it is your children, your spouse, your dog, your garden—take a nice deep breath and visualize those things that make life good for you. Put down deep roots for nourishment and stability.

Take a tip from our elder kindred, the trees, and sink your roots down deep in this time of lengthening day. Remember who and what you are, and find all the ways that nourish that be-ing.

And we went on to the ancient excuse for alcohol, song, and dance as we practiced the wonderful old ritual of wassailing. Wassailing is the custom of wishing good health for your kith and kin and even your apple trees.

The word wassail comes from the Saxon and is a greeting meaning "be in good health" or literally "be whole." There are several different traditions of wassailing, depending on the culture or area. The point of wassailing is to bestow your own charm or spell for good health and fertility in the coming growing season, and in the case of those sleeping apples trees, it's a way to honor the tree spirits and bless the trees in the hope of a good growing season and bountiful harvest.

I invited each one to turn to their neighbor and wish them health and prosperity in the coming year. And then I spoke the words for going.

Benediction

> *May you have dew for a blessing.*
> *And abundant rain*
> *for water is a need of all green and growing things,*
> *every plant and tree.*
> *Make deep our roots*
> *and wide our crowns,*
> *that we may blossom in season and bring forth*
> *our fruits of goodness and of beauty.*
> *We ask the Ancient Ones to strengthen our hands and our*
> *backs*
> *and give us hearts to revive the sacred soil.*
> *Our oldest Mother.*
> *So mote it be. Blessed be.*

In my travels, I often talk with people who tell me how lucky I am to have a strong Pagan community. We're not so much lucky as we are stubborn. We have spent a quarter of a century—a generation—building this wibbly-wobbly community brick by brick. And first we made the bricks. You can do that too.

It takes courage, hard work, vision, dedication—and mountains of stubbornness. A community is a living, breathing thing that must be fed and loved. As you claim the authority to create ways of honoring the changes that are rolling through the culture, you will find many ways, small and large, to create and feed and love your community to strength and health.

CHAPTER THREE

FILTH AND GRIME AND WOMAN AND EARTH

The connections between and among women are the most feared, the most problematic, and the most potentially transforming force on the planet.
—Adrienne Rich

CIRCLE CAST

Here is the Mystery.
Thus is the Spiral set—
Four elemental goddesses hold the sacred precinct.
Three quarters are Earth and Air and Fire,
with the Womblike Waters holding the Center.
Two then are You and She.
One is the Center, the Union of All That Is.
Spiral in, spiral out.
Thus is our spiral set.

Sometimes it feels we have come to the point of no return. The statistics about global climate change are sobering. The number of hungry, homeless, and addicted children is horrifying in such a land of plenty. Political conservatives demand a return to a world that never existed—where everything was sweet and calm and beautiful. In reality it was unequal and unjust.

These changeable and confusing days have knocked many of us off center as we endure the grief of blighted expectations, the anger that comes from our frustrating lack of agency. Perhaps the first thing we all can do is to remember a time when we felt hope and envisioned a world with some possibilities for improvement. But some of us have never felt that, you protest, and that is true. As we consciously put together these new days, this new time, we can listen to each other where we are. And those of us who have the experience of hope can share the dream of it through story and song and the uses of magic with its brightest and darkest enchantments.

Let's return together, friends. Return to our strong and vital selves. Return to a time when we laughed loudly, when we could laugh at ourselves as well as the madness around us. Perhaps you start by blessing the grocery store bagger who put the bread on the bottom of your bag, under the almond milk. Bless that person who disagrees with you about politics—even if their language is rough and illogical and a little frightening. Bless yourself in the morning as you go through your begin-the-day routine. We can dance our way through this, in a great circle, setting aside the little differences for a greater and—more blessed—whole. It's not like the Macarena—your future self won't be embarrassed by your dance moves with this particular dance. Start now, with yourself. Place your strongest hand over your heart, and murmur some words of blessing. And if it feels right, give some of that to your neighbor or your partner or your colleague.

Blessing, being blessed—the sacred give-and-take that is healing as well as empowering.

I worked for many years in nonprofit arts management, and we came to understand the best way to tackle big impossible projects. We'd sit in staff meetings and remind each other of something we'd learned in one of dozens of workshops we'd organized over the years.

How do you eat an elephant? One bite at a time.

Let's take a bite of the elephant that is our American life, and let's do that together to secure our resilience in these chaotic times. A tiny step into freedom from fear, a wee dance step into the circle we all long to create. Time to fly, sisters and brothers. We have been too long looking down, fearing the day. We don't have time to dillydally or fret about things we can't fix. Time to figure out what needs fixing and see if we have the tools to do it. I suspect we do. Because I obviously believe we stand at a pivotal place in history.

And I reckon people have been thinking the same thing since time immemorial.

But in these potential dark ages—unlike the original Dark Ages—we are connected through all sorts of strands of information, much of it electronic. We have facts and information at the touch of a screen, but I suspect we're none of us as adept as we should be at weaving all that gibberish together to form real thought, genuine vision.

So what can we do as we explore the renewal and revivification of our life-force? What can we do to shake off despair and remember joy? Like some ancient indigenous people did, we can work together to erect great and symbolic earth works, the equivalent of Silbury Hill or Avebury. Hill forts, barrows, mounds, banks and ditches—these earthen fortifications, for this fan of Neolithic archaeology, seemed like a natural conceit for this book.

Here are some simple, cultural "earthen fortifications" to consider adding to your work-basket.

Grounding (also called "earthing," interestingly enough) is one good exercise for reconnecting our little selves to the forces of the great big universe.

You can do a guided meditation to take you to a solid place. Imagine that roots grow out through the bottoms of your feet and into the deep, rich soil of the earth. Feel that nourishment and nurturing, knowing you are a part and not apart.

Connect with your family and community in real and simple and sweet ways; take time out for picnics and trips to the movies. Plant a row of lettuce together in the front yard, water and tend it. Draw those you love close, and let those whom you honor know that. Share your extra radishes or cucumbers with the neighbor you barely know.

What can you suggest for grounding yourself in the heart of community? How are you turning away from despair and rage and finding equilibrium in this time of change?

When I look at the circles of women that have nurtured me throughout my spiritual life, I understand that I came of age spiritually in a strange and invigorating time, a time when the leaders of the local communities were mostly women like me. Women like these were probably the religious leaders in your local community if you came up in the 1970s and 1980s.

I light three candles on my altar most mornings, take deep breaths and meditate on life lived in service to a plurality of female Divines. I am now an ordained high priestess, and I live my life in the lap of the Goddess.

To be a priestess in this way is to be empowered by the Divine Feminine all around us. It is to know that time moves in a never-ending spiral of energy and intention. It is seeing the Mother's face in the world all around us—in the elements of Gaia, the darkness of Hecate, the wildness of Kali.

First and foremost, we envision Earth that birthed and nourishes us as female. We revel in all aspects of life on the planet and feel unbounding joy in living a Pagan life. The Earth is our mother and sister, but perhaps more exactly, she is our grandmother. Wise, ancient, full of deep mysteries and ultimately unknowable. We honor her as home, as womb, as matrix of all life. We also respect her as an immensely complex system that is constantly engaged in the dual act of creation and destruction. This is an awe-inspiring power with which we are suitably awed.

Structurally, the spirituality I practice is affirmingly nonhierarchical. Consensus building is a conscious part of our decision-making and our spiritual practice.

Group magical workings are only undertaken with the unanimous consent of the workers. We meet in circles, groves, or covens, and our work is as inclusive of all present as possible. A high priestess often functions as the ritualist of the group and as group mother. A priestess may work with a priestess-in-training, or she may work at the altar alone. Our rituals often include a talking stick with which we check in, honoring the speech of our circle sisters and brothers as they tell where they are (both emotionally and physically) at the time of the ritual.

As many Pagans do, I follow the cycle of the agricultural year. Most of us end and begin the year at Samhain when the Goddess in her aspect as Crone/ Grandmother reaches the height of her power.

We believe that the Earth is all sacred space, and we refer to the cast circle as "ritual" or "intentional" space, being mindful that every space is sacred.

We acknowledge that centuries of living under an autocratic and misogynistic culture has left gaping wounds in the human psyche. We accept that we must all be healers as well as ritualists, that we must salve spirits that are hurting and feed those that are hungry. We do this through ritual as well as activism on behalf of oppressed people within our own communities.

We believe in rearing our children in our spirituality, and we honor their transitions in several rituals. Following the birth of a new member of our clan family, we hold a ritual called a saining, in which the child is presented to the Goddess, to the Ancestors, to the spirits of the place, and to the clan family. When our children reach puberty, we ritualize the moment with the First Blood for girls and Green Manning for boys. In this rite, we accept them as young adults in the group.

Our other rites of passage include handfasting, when we unite loving persons through an intentional bonding ceremony. We mark eldering through a Croning or Maging ritual. And we bid our beloved dead bon voyage to Tir Nan Og with funerary rites and acts of ritual mourning. We do other rites of passage as they arise. A woman with children gone to college might need a special celebration. A man who has lost a job may need something else entirely.

We acknowledge a great debt to our ancient forebears, to those who lost their lives, properties, and will during the European Inquisitions and to the people who kept alive a glowing ember of the Goddess through generations of Christian veneer. We thank those people who worshipped the Goddess in her aspect as Mary (along with all the saints) as well as those who kept their ancestral and household deities, passing them (often in secret) to the next generation. We also thank the women and men in the early 60s and 70s who gave the modern American Pagan movement its firm foundation.

From Inanna (my personal matron) and the Goddess of Laussel, from Malta to Africa to the Ring of Fire onward through the priestesses and warriors of classical times through the midwives of Europe and America and into the present day where we enjoy, at last, the return of the Goddess in Her glory. This is our history as we see it. A wide web, a long thread that reaches back from the modern priestess standing at her American altar to our ancestors at the dawn of human time. A connection that has been strained and frayed but never truly broken.

This is the life of a priestess—the philosophy, the liturgy. But I also balance that with the homely practices that have come to be called witchcraft, the craft that writer Terry Pratchett refers to as "hagging." Hagging and witchery are probably the same thing, but I think of hagging (i.e. Hagia Sophia) as acquired wisdom made manifest and witchery as something you whip up in your kitchen. Maybe it boils down to a theatrical convention— witchery requires props and ingredients, hagging just requires force of will.

When creating ceremonies and rituals, it's wise to base them in the participants' biosphere or position them as rites of passage. The following cast was first used in a harvest ritual. The cast is centered on seasonal grains.

North: I remember how the seed heads, tanned from the sun, stand in the wide fields near the river. I remember the threshing of the grain and the stretching stomachs it fills. I remember the bowl, with butter and sugar, and a man dressed as a friend. In this time of the grain harvest, I call the Ancestors and the Guardians of the North with the strength of oats! You are welcome at our table!

East: I have planted the flat kernels in mounds the width of my hand. I have seen the shocking green of the stalks as they rise. The oldest peoples put a fish's head in the mound to feed the proud green shoots. Tall spears to hold the other sister. In this time of the grain harvest, I call the Ancestors and Guardians of the East with the bright yellow kernels of corn! You are welcome at our table!

South: I sing now of the fire of the sun, of the loaf made edible through the flailing of the grain. I sing now of the bright fire of food that is enduring, of food that is beautiful to see. I sing of grains that feed the people and straw that makes the bricks. In this time of the grain harvest, I call the Ancestors and Guardians of the South with the banked fire of wheat! You are welcome at our table!

West: I create a necklace of the pearls of barley. I create soup from the waters of the sea and the tears of my kindred who passed into the West. I create the living vision of a shining new world. I create a passageway for my descendants to greet my Ancestors. In this time of the grain harvest, I call the Ancestors and Guardians of the West with the perfect jewels of barley! You are welcome at our table!

Invocation

> *Come, Beautiful Mother*
> *Come, Loving Grandmother*
> *Come, Happy Sister*
> *Join our dance,*
> *sing with us our song.*
> *Thank you!*
> *For the harvest, for the rain,*
> *for the love.*
> *Thank you!*
> *Thank you!*

Devocation/Release

Go with thanks and go with blessing, sweet Lady of the gardens, Lady of the pastures, Lady of the orchards. Or stay, for you are in our hearts always.

Circle Cast: Autumn Equinox

The following cast was created for the second harvest at the autumnal equinox. It features seasonal fruits and vegetables common to the southern Appalachian Mountains.

North: I call the elementals of the North through the solid, enduring beauty of winter squash. The bold vines leap across the Earth, joyous in yellow blossoms—the joy of bees!—and then the fruits are born beneath the leaves, solid, bold, enduring. Elemental power of the North, we call you forth!

East: I call the elementals of the East through the sharp and succulent kernels of mountain-grown corn. Three little seeds go into the hill, and the mature stalks reach beyond the head of a tall woman. And the silk! So soft, so abundant—we strip back the husk to reveal all the colors of the earth, sharp, soft, plentiful. Elemental powers of the East, we call you forth!

South: I call the elementals of the South through the heavy, fiery juices of pumpkin. Who can know how large they will grow? The small green globes speed their way to maturity, and the light from their carved faces bring joy to all on a dark night. The fires of the cookstove brown the crust and set the custard of pie. Heavy, fiery, light. Elemental powers of the South, we call you forth!

West: I call the elementals of the West in the varieties and crispness of apples. Tended orchards and backyard swings, the red, green, and yellow apples fall with a thud, awaiting what comes. Bite them, bake them, plant the seeds! Most beloved of all fruits! And when pressed into service as cider, sweet or hard—delight! Red, crispness, delight. Elemental powers of the West, we call you forth!

So you see how you can adopt a fairly traditional circle-form ritual for the needs of your community.

Smaller, more personal rites of passage can also be ceremonialized, and many of these transitions are easy when placed into a format that allows for divine participation, as well as the participation of the human community. There are so many things to celebrate, to mark the passages of individuals and in communities and to acknowledge your place in the biosphere.

CHAPTER FOUR

ALTARS OF CLOUD

Let Appalachia rise.
I believe in the justice of the Ancestors.
I believe in the wisdom of the hills and hollers.
I believe in the strength of the people.
Let Appalachia rise!
I swear by my granny's apron.
I swear by the cool sweet water.
I swear by the blood of my people.
Let Appalachia rise.
Let Appalachia rise!
—a prayer following devastating
wildfires in southern Appalachia

Appalachia, the southern highlands of it, is my home—the place I write about and live in and love. My first two books were a celebration of the folk magic of this place where my deep, gnarly roots continue to grow. Every day I get to spend in my garden or in the woods or by the old French Broad River is a day that tucks me further into myself and makes me, once again, exactly who I am.

We are a complicated culture here, irascible and independent. Proud and stubborn and generous. Xenophobic, violent, tender. Balancing all that this culture has and can be, the settling into my "simple country woman" persona seems at times inauthentic and at other times completely true.

As with everything we explore in these Tower Times, it is wise to learn this about ourselves and the cultures we hold (and the world in general)—most things are not the one thing nor the other. They are a combination of traditions and histories and resources, and it is difficult to tease out the purity of any one thing.

I can be a traveler and a woman with a terminal degree in my academic field and a redneck and a witch—and so many other things. All of you are the same. You are not one thing, none of you. You are a complex weaving of events and inclinations and histories. Because you acknowledge that and you have the presence of mind to honor the same thing in all the people that you meet, you have a chance to be at home in the whole of the world and to find companions and allies in odd and unbelievable places. So that no one is unknowable to you nor any situation immediately impossible.

This chapter is about re-sacralizing home and the simplicity that used to be called homeliness. We'll explore home and homeliness and being at home in a tectonic world. It is about altars big and small and about keeping the energy flowing in your home and your life. I'll offer you some techniques and protocols that you may find helpful because I am finding that many people are not instructed in any clear way about these simple practices. These times ask much of the place we call home and invite you to claim your place as a citizen of the world.

There really is no place like home, but many of us live in a place that is more battlefield than gentle bower. The sort of simple folk magic we practice here in the southern highlands may be helpful in sweetening your living space and giving you the sort of nest from which you can be both happy and effective in the world.

Tidying and dusting and generally clearing up is always a good place to start, but you may be too bummed out to do that first. So I am going to suggest that if you can't clear up the tangibles, you clear the energy first, and that will give the inspiration to clean up the house. Clearing the space in this way is about moving energy around, flowing gently with the rhythms of your life.

Feng shui is an Eastern science that is designed to identify and correct the movement of energy in an enclosed space. We do something like that here too, though it's more instinctive and less formal. I believe what we do may be based on some old English customs that traveled with us when we emigrated from the motherland to this brave new world in America.

When our community gathers together, we sometimes sing this song:

We all are here.
We all are here.
All manner of good things
will come to us now.

I use that little song in many places for many things, and it always serves to ground a group in the place they stand at the moment so that we can move on from there to a more productive and deeper place. I murmur it to myself when I begin a difficult job of work. When I do a house cleansing and blessing these days, I add that song at the end. The home-dwellers and I stand in a circle and sing this, invoking the sweet spirit of place into the shining energy of the house. Do you do a blessing on your home when you first move in or have someone else do that for you? Do you pause at the doorway—that perfectly liminal place—and speak softly: Bless this place and all who enter here?

No?

Let's begin there in the spirit of blessing.

The notion of "home" is fraught with meaning, loaded with memory, lost in the dreamland between our actual lives and our fantasy ones. From an Airstream trailer retreat in grandma's backyard to a ruined keep in the Scottish Highlands, from a ragged apartment in public housing to a comfy brownstone in a gentrified historic section of the city, most of us want to have a place that we call home. Even those intentional nomads among us want a nest to return to, a place where we can leave our stuff, change our socks, recharge the electronics.

A place so significant and close to our hearts must by necessity require our magical attention. In this essay, we'll look at protecting our hearths, gaining the trust of allies, and contemplating those residents who have gone on to their rewards but somehow remain in situ. All of this will come through the lens of my own Appalachian practice and be illustrated by my own experiences.

I grew up hearing stories of my great-grandmother's home, long gone now but once standing just down the hill from my house. Its number was also its name, and it loomed large in the family mythology of my childhood. Number Ten Roberts Street was a wooden two-story building, the bottom of which was a general store. The family lived upstairs. As did the ghost who slept on the couch, if one can say that a ghost lives somewhere. My mother always supposed that it was an odd trick of the streetlight that caused the family to see a man sleeping on the couch in the hallway upstairs. Because it wasn't Grandpa or one of the boys. It was someone who wasn't actually there.

When I go to do a house clearing or a blessing, the first thing I do upon arrival is to recognize the land spirits and give them an offering of food and drink. My little black house call bag has a couple of oyster-shucking knives in it, and I'll use one of them to dig a hole in the yard. Some brightly colored treats—usually some kind of gummi candy—go into the hole, and I pour a shot of alcohol on top before filling the hole with dirt. Whether you are going to someone's house to do work or bulking up the general contentment of your own hearthside, acknowledging the spirits of yard and house are important.

If you have moved to a new part of the country or to a new house in the same town, please take time to acquaint yourself with what Eddie Lenihan calls "the Other Crowd" and Michael Smith calls "the Locals." These are some of your most important allies in learning the lay of your new land. Walk through the yard, if there is one, and listen, observe. Is there a particular place that feels lively to you? A gnarled old tree? Add a stone or two and use that as the place where you leave regular offerings for the land spirits. Experiment a bit and see what seems to be best accepted. Cream and other dairy products are traditional, but you may find they like strong coffee and toast with butter or the aforementioned candy and alcohol.

In many parts of the South, especially in older houses, the ceiling of the porch is painted a very light blue. Sometimes you'll be told that it keeps insects away in the summer or that mud daubers won't build on it or that it makes the porch seem cooler in the long evenings of a Southern summer. But that particular shade of blue is not called "Carolina blue." It's called "haint blue" and originates with the Low Country Gullah people, as I understand it. It is there to shield your house from ghosts and other walking spirits. Period. The rest is just meringue on the pie. Set dressing.

As I go about the region doing fieldwork, I ask folks about the odd things they remember their elders doing. Houses and barns usually got a horseshoe above the doorways, always turned up in a U shape, to collect luck and hold it. To turn it the other way is to let your luck run out. A piece of lightning-struck wood may grace a fireplace or be nailed to the side of the barn with a handmade nail. A kitchen windowsill might hold a chipped canning jar with bits of broken glass in it. Some of the glass might be the green of a 7 Up bottle, the blue of a Vicks VapoRub jar, and so it is a kind of pretty stained glass oddment. The little jar's real purpose, though, is to confound any wandering ne'er-do-well spirits, who will have to stop at the window and count each of the broken edges.

Modern magical practitioners may think in terms of warding the entire property, and here's one way you can do that. I use flat glass beads—the ones found in floral arrangements—to set the wards. If possible, I bury them at the corners of the property, and then I raise a circle of energy going from bead to bead. I attach the circle to a tree or boulder and let that natural feature hold the circle in place. Then I renew the circle every month on the waxing moon.

Here is a basic house cleansing with added attention paid to any unseen residents. I ask the homeowner to open all doors and windows if possible. I leave an offering outside for the land spirits and then spend a few minutes of quiet time, explaining to an unseen resident that it is time to go on home to her family. If I know her name, I address her by name. I usually do this silently and finish by announcing aloud—time to do the house.

I walk through the house, starting at the front door. I carry a pot of sweet smoke, using my open hand to waft it into all the corners. I do every room—front to back, basement to attic. I pass through the house a second time, this time ringing a large bell. I used to use my great-grandmother's dinner bell, but I bought a small cowbell a few years ago, and that sets up a racket, which is a good thing. Often I'll ask the owners to step outside because the effects of the ringing can be unpleasant. In fact, if you do this very often, you may want to use ear protection yourself. I keep green earplugs in my little black bag.

I do a third and final pass-through in which I dab a drop of oil on the doorjambs, windowsills, fireplace, sinks—all the openings into (and out of) the house that I can reach. I do this one slowly too, and I begin again at the front door by placing my hand on the side of the open door and saying firmly, "Bless this house and all who enter here."

When I have finished all the dressing work, I go to stand at the back door and wish the departing spirit a loving farewell and a safe journey home. Let me stress that this can take a couple of hours to do properly— longer if you are inexperienced—and you don't want to do a lick-and-a-promise job here. You can also invite the homeowner to stand with you for the final farewell part. That can be surprisingly touching, and involving the new resident will help them establish their claim to be the only resident.

Another tactic I've used is a trap made out of a jar with a lid, half-filled with soil. I have found this to be especially useful with an unknown or disruptive spirit energy. Depending on the size of the job, I set up the jar in the lowest point of the building that I can access. I place a battery-operated tea light candle on top of the soil, and then I spend my quiet time as outlined above. I leave the jar open for three or seven days, depending on my schedule and the size of the job. I do ask the resident to check on it daily and replace the tea light if it burns out. At the end of that time, I place the lid on the jar as tightly as it can be twisted. I remove the jar of soil with the tea light fading out and take the whole thing to a suitable cemetery, where I pour the soil out at the edge of the cemetery. I take the jar and tea light with me, leaving only some soil behind and in an out-of-the-way place.

I developed the Energy Trap many years ago, and it has proved to be very effective. It acts as a kind of HEPA filter for stagnant energy in your home, energy that can be misconstrued as spirit activity. Here are directions for constructing and using one.

You'll need a flat, round reflective surface (the bottom of a throwaway pie pan is the best, but you can use a round mirror too), three flat black rocks, a tea light candle (my preference is a battery-operated one because they are safe around children and animals), and two grades of salt (inexpensive table salt and ice cream salt, for instance).

Place the reflective surface on a flat surface—put it on a high shelf out of sight if that's needed, or put it in a prominent place to add the energy of your thoughts every time you see it. Put the three flat stones in the center of the mirror. Pour the rough salt in a circle around the stones. Pour the table salt on the outer edge of the mirror. Now place the tea light on top of the stones in the center and light it or turn it on.

The theory behind this trap is that stagnant and unhealthy energy is drawn to the light, filtered first through the stones, then filtered through the rough salt, filtered a final time through the fine salt. It is then reflected back out into the area as clean, usable energy.

You can keep one of these going all the time, but it isn't necessary. You'll feel the difference in a few days. If you are moving into a new place or if your office environment is harsh, run the trap for at least a moon cycle. If you run it longer than that, change the salt every moon cycle.

There are so many Divines who hold the office of hearth keeper in their pantheon and in the hearts of their people. Let us join them and our spirit allies in cherishing and tending our home places. This attention is important for our spiritual practices as much as our well-being. Whether you own your place or rent it, if you live in a tiny flat, a trailer, or a mansion, you will find that keeping the energy sweet and flowing in your domicile will be a blessing to you, your family, and your neighbors. It is one aspect of nurturing community that is often left out of our general discussions, and I encourage you to give it a try.

Technically, an altar is a place of sacrifice. A home altar is a place of commemoration and a place to sit quietly for your meditative spiritual practice. It need not be elaborate and can even be what I refer to as a "stealth altar"—a simple table arrangement that is easy to gaze upon. Altars can be small and personal or large and communal or anything in between. It is the place where you consciously connect with the Divines and where you honor that connection with offerings, with sacred decoration, and with ritual.

I often advise you to consider a regular spiritual practice that both grounds and focuses you. As we work through the challenges of our age, giving yourself the gift of this practice is important.

Whether you light a candle and chant or pray while wreathed in incense smoke or clear every worry and anxious thought from your busy mind, a regular meditative practice will benefit you. Daily practices change and grow over time. I have found for myself that I sometimes add an evening meditation to my morning one when times are especially stressful. Don't be afraid to do things seasonally, to develop a particular part of your practice for your own moon time or for a moon phase. It can be a simple or a wonderfully creative activity.

Find a comfortable place to sit, a place you will be undisturbed for five minutes. Could be a bath in the evening, a morning cup of tea. Sit down, put your feet flat on the floor, and take a moment to ground and center yourself. Take a deep belly breath—slow inhale, pause, slow exhale, pause. If you'd like to count that out, try to breathe in on a count of ten, rest for five, breathe out for ten, rest for five. Repeat this four times. At this point you may want to close your eyes and give yourself permission to do only this thing for a few moments. You may also want to set a timer if you are in a morning time crunch. Breathe in and out, and listen to what your body is telling you. Open your eyes and sip your tea if you are doing a cuppa tea meditation. While in this balanced state, consider lighting a candle or repeating a prayer or poem.

Sit and breathe and think. Quiet your mind, listen to your body, but don't try to blank everything out. We want to practice being in the world and informed by the spaces and spirits around us. Five minutes, once a day, for one week.

The following are two prayers I adapted from Alexander Carmichael's Carmina Gadelica. The first is for the morning, the second for a bedtime meditation.

In Brigid's Keeping

Each night and each day,
I speak the blessing of Brigid.
I am under the shielding of
Good Brigid each day.
I am under the shielding of
Good Brigid each night.
I am under her keeping,
early and late, every dark, every light.
Brigid is my companion,
Brigid is my maker of song,
Brigid is my helping-woman,
My guide, my friend.

Bed Blessing Before Sleep

In the name of Brigid,
I stand above my pillow—
Sweetened with lavender and roses.
I stand above my pillow, and I bless my head
In the name of Brigid.
I touch my blanket—
Sweetened in the fresh breezes of the morn's dawning,
I touch my blanket and
I bless my body
In the name of Brigid.
I sit upon my bed—
Sweetened with visions of bliss and good health.
I sit upon my bed and
I bless my sleeping
In the name of Brigid.

Sacred Smoke

I make a special kind of smudge that is Appalachian in origin but not traditional. The ingredients are mountain mint (pycnanthemum virginianum), rabbit tobacco (pseudognaphalium obtusifolium), mugwort (artemesia vulgaris), in equal amounts of each, all dried naturally but not so dry that the oils have gone. I have a little cast-iron pan, and I burn it in there, sometimes on a charcoal round and sometimes just burning a pile of the dried herbs. I call it "sweet smoke."

Sweetening the space with sweet smoke and fresh herbs begins with opening the doors and windows and letting in some fresh air. I advise folks to do this and then stand in the open doorway facing out. In this way you claim authority over your space and take responsibility for improving it. It's especially effective if you stand in the doorway with your hands on your hips.

Then walk through the house with the sweet smoke and let it waft into all the corners of the rooms. Corners can be gnarly little places and benefit from your attention. Make sure and smoke all the entrances and exits—including where electricity and water come in.

Dressing the Entryways with Sweet Oil

After the smoke, return to the front door and place a drop of olive oil—which in earlier times was called sweet oil—on the doorframe. I add a blessing at this point, saying softly, "Bless this house and all who enter here." Continue through the house, leaving a tiny smear of sweet oil at each window and door, saying "Bless this house."

We like to think of the hearth as the heart of any home—the central place where our cold hands and bottoms can warm up in front of a cheery fire. Most of us don't have a literal hearth or fireplace and must consider the hearth an ancient metaphor of ingathering and hospitality. We can call the image of homely fire to use in many ways. What follows is a circle cast that honors the warmth and brightness of this powerful element. You will notice that it begins in the South, which in much modern Pagan practice is the placement of the element of fire. It was originally used in a winter solstice ritual.

Circle Cast: Honoring the Hearth Fire

South: I call out to the living fire of the South and invoke its power in bonfires and cook-fires, in soft candlelight and fierce conflagration. Bearing both heat and light, contained in the woodstove, feral on the dry autumn hills. Warm fires of the South, we honor you this solstice night. Be welcome!

West: I call out to the liquid West and invoke its power in the oils that feed fire. Coal oil pulled from the face of the mountains, kerosene lamps to read in the evening, tallow of slaughters to light the way. Western flame of lamp and heater, we honor you this solstice night. Be welcome!

North: I call out to the solid North and invoke its power in the hot springs of the far mountains. A microclimate sweetened by the fiery heart of the Earth herself. Steam and wrinkled fingers, cares are left in the healing waters of the hot springs. Beautiful North, we honor you this solstice night. Be welcome!

East: I call out to the mists of the Smoky Mountains and invoke the power of the smoke of campfire and burning leaves. The wind carries the smells to us from miles away, gathering all the scents—of wet earth and skunk and incense on the altar. Deep breath of East, we honor you this solstice night. Be welcome!

Release

East: We watch the woodsmoke move along the valley, always following beauty. Grandmothers of the East, go if you must. But lend us your scent of freedom a while longer if you will. So may it be.

North: We feel the hot water soothe our aching feet and backs and soothe our anxious souls. Grandmothers of the North, go if you must. But lend us a moment longer in the hot tubs if you will. So may it be.

West: We wind down the wick and extinguish the flame. Grandmothers of the West, go if you must. But lend us your light a while longer if you will. So may it be.

South: We stir the coals and bank down the hearth fire. Grandmothers of the South, go if you must. But lend us your warmth on this cold night awhile longer if you will. So may it be.

CHAPTER FIVE

THE BLINDNESS OF WORMS

One thing I love about her
is the way she keeps her house
There's a candle in every window
and a bed for every mouse
The birds in the backyard bathing
stop and listen to her prose
As each word escapes her lips
hangs in the air and softly glows
And when she's done she reads her book
beside a crackling fire
And slips into the Land of Nod
where truth becomes desire
Yes, I love the way she keeps her house
where in beauty she does reside
Look through her windows to the Universe
Her doors of love are open wide

—Brian Henke, "Love Song for Terra."

We don't like to use the word "judgment" because it implies we think we're better than other people and have the authority to trivialize or dismiss their lives and opinions and experiences from our lofty superior position. The acceptable word for those processes is "discernment." Whichever word you choose to use, it may be important to sharpen this skill in these fraught times.

Judging was not a skill that came naturally to me. For many years I could tell you the differences between two things, but I couldn't tell if one was superior to the other. I was and am observant but was not discerning, mostly because I didn't know I had the right to decide what I did and didn't like. As I worked on knowing myself better, I was able to decide between two things, after observing their similarities and differences.

We judge things constantly. Am I following too close to the car in front of me? Yes. Slow down. Her hair was really cute short. Why is she growing it out? It looks stringy and unhealthy. What he said hurt my feelings. Did he mean that the way I heard it? Or am I in a weird place, feeling unappreciated and disrespected?

Sharpening our observation skills, figuring out what we genuinely prefer, and knowing those things that nourish and nurture us—these are helpful tools for our work-baskets. These tools can also help us in weaving the resilient communities we desire and that may sustain our species in times to come.

What follows is a love song for dear annelida (earthworms), those blind and necessary beings beloved of all gardeners. When my daughter was very small (and would still hang out with me when I was in the garden), I found a stellar example of these folks and gasped in delight. She wanted to see, of course, and I put the soft body into the palm of her soft hand. She took it between the thumb and forefinger of her other hand and raised it up like a string of spaghetti, but I retrieved it before she could eat it. In her defense, she was about two years old and I had been handing her things to eat for many months.

Why earthworms for this chapter of thought and potentially useful suggestions? Perhaps because it is important to look at the efforts of seemingly humble acts and to emulate them. We can peer at earthworms and blindness and ponder the idea that we can feel our way through some of these challenges and be successful. As with most of this book, it is also an invitation for you to widen your concepts of holiness and worthiness.

What Is More Sacred Than Earthworms? A Paean

Taking a break from writing, surrounded by seed catalogs and looking askance at the dirt under my nails, I am contemplating the realms of the holy.

It's the dirt part that's done it.

We're preparing the garden for spring planting. In a usual year, I would have planted onions in the January thaw, and we'd be eating fat, glossy spinach that wintered over. We would have radishes too—beautiful earthen rubies with their feathered caps.

But the intense cold of this early season has flattened the spinach and baby carrots and stung the little radishes. When they thaw, they may be okay, but they may be too winter damaged to be edible. The soil in the raised beds is hard as iron, and no onions can be planted. It has been an unusual winter for us here in the southern highlands.

In preparing the gardens for their seasonal fallow time—back before the deep freeze set in—we moved a considerable pile of last fall's leaves, and therein lay the holiness I contemplated as I looked at my chipped fingernails.

Earthworms. Fat, red, glorious in their industry.

Holy, holy, holy!

Surely there is an earthworm deity in someone's pantheon. Did our Ancestors not realize the incredible importance of these wandering lovers, who eat and poop and aerate the soil?

I wonder what such a deity would look like—a winged and wet serpent? A sea monster? A beautiful, fat pink baby?

My heart leaps with joy when I turn the soil and see them there, busy in their blindness. They seem a greater harbinger of spring than any simple robin. Those wigglers are redolent of life and loam, of transformation and possibility.

When I peruse the delights of catalogs—where each flower and vegetable is bright and effortless—I smile to think of the roots in the soil. I ponder the magic of hard seeds growing into impossibly large plants, bearing their fruits for my nourishment.

Sun and rain are the visible components of the peppers and tomatoes that I love. But the real heroes, the tiny and silent movers, are the earthworms that do what they do in such a simple and—dare I say?—elegant way.

They are a blessing and an ornament. May your garden be richly blessed with their saintliness. May your life be so industriously lived with such a generous result.

As I am often driven to do, I've created a circle cast and release that follows and gives homage to these important and common creatures and to the world garden they inhabit. Feel free to use it for a private ceremony or a community berm... or as you approach the beginning of your agricultural year.

Circle Cast: Honoring the Earthworms

North: I honor the North through the marvelous earthworm. Blind and hopeful, moving through the dark and moist of the world, always searching, always finding. Making soil through your castings, you are humble, elegant, perfect, the garden's friend, the birds' delight. You fling yourself, little cousin, onto the asphalt pathways, avoiding the new rain—drawn up from your perfect tunnels into the air and the light of the sky. Welcome, earthworms!

East: I honor the East through the power of dirt. What is better in all the world than the smell of earth as it begins to rain? How can we love this stuff enough? We use it up, we make it, we ignore it, we adore it. It's under our nails and on our feet; it is the very ground of all existence. Rich, loamy, friable, precious, microbe-filled; the brown skirt of our oldest kin, wide and welcome grandmother. Welcome, dirt!

South: I honor the South through the fickleness of rain. Come back, little sister, we miss you. You have been too long in the Midwest, and we need you to pay a visit to us here. The rivers are longing for you, the old apple trees are tired of shedding their green fruit because you are playing so hard-to-get. We love your light touch, your blessing, even your faithlessness. Splash, little sister, through our lives, making us puddles of summer glory. Welcome, rain!

West: I honor the West through the infinity of seeds. We were all seeds once. So were trees and beets and corn. Those little crusty bits of life, the little mothers. You are the multitude of beginnings. We cast you forth to the wind and the earth and the rain and to life. Burrow your hard self into the bosom of our dear mother and bring forth all that we are, all that we need, all that we dream. Large in possibility, small in size. We welcome seeds!

Release

West: Little mothers on the wind and in the soil, clutched in the fur of the cat, blown by a child from the head of a spent weed. Remain with us as a blessing if you will—leave us to travel with your bounty over the whole of the dear Earth if you must. Blessed be!

South: Little sister, call our name! Speak to us on the tin roof and in the rain barrel as you drip from the branches above. We love your going, and we love your arrival. Stay for a while and then go your way, as if we can tell you what to do. Blessed be!

East: We want you to stay and not fly away on the dry wind, not flow in mud down embankments to silt up the creeks. Stay in your thickness and richness, and if you must go, let us share you with our neighbors as bags of black gold, the most precious thing on Earth. Blessed be!

North: Little cousins, be with us always. Let us find you in the garden and under the compost. But go where you must, doing what you do, knowing our love and respect go with you. Blessed be!

ᚲᚱᚺᛋᚾ

As you deepen your understanding of yourself, your people, and the world around you, you may choose to be more public in the work you do as a way to gather support and to weave this new world we keep talking about. You will then be called upon to help in small and large ways.

As the self-styled village witch in my little town and a very public Pagan, I often receive messages, sad phone calls, and sometimes despairing emails. Often these emails go out to an entire list, so it's not a personal request.

There is a depressing sameness about those notes and calls, an unwelcome vista into someone's private world. It's a world that is peopled with sickness and poverty, with poor choices and a lack of personal responsibility.

Let me be clear—this isn't about the person whose world has genuinely fallen apart, someone who needs a helping hand or a listening ear. This is about those people who can never manage any sort of organization, who are always in crisis mode, who are a drain on everyone around them all the time.

And how often does a similar request arrive from the same person, someone who can't seem to get his life in order, can't seem to keep a job or be agreeable to her coven mates? Sometimes the details are slightly different, but the request is always the same. Help me. I don't know what to do. I am at my wits' end! Why is my life always like this? Wah wah wah.

These requests often come from people you barely know, from friends of friends. "Light a candle and send some energy because my life is a total mess!"

There are always a multitude of exclamation points and emoticons to drive the point home. The request for a candle is often part of the general plea.

Okay, it's easy enough to light a candle, but without the necessary work that goes with it, all it does is give a little light and heat and suck up valuable oxygen.

Inevitably, when I ask about daily spiritual practice, the petitioner hems and haws and finally says they either don't have an altar or a daily practice or they are "too stressed" to do it. One actually told me that her altar was on top of the TV and her kids kept messing with it, so she put it away.

Away.

Mothers of gods.

"Send energy." Do they have any idea how hard that is? No, they don't. Because all this is symbolic for those people, they don't actually raise energy or utilize energy. If they did, they couldn't possibly ask someone they don't know to do such a thing.

If we say we are magic workers, if we have a relationship with Ancestors and Deities, surely the first thing you do is "pray harder."

In working with some of those lost souls, I've begun to develop a list of things to do when you are in dire need, when you are reaching out for the umpteenth time to people you don't know, people you perceive to be stronger than you, more together than you.

Those people may have problems they are working out privately, or they may indeed know the secret to making life work. Those paragons of Pagan virtue probably have a daily spiritual practice that keeps them grounded and focused. When life starts to interfere with their stuff, they buckle down and do any or all of the following, and this is my advice when the exclamation points attack.

Go outside and activate the spirits of the land on which you live. This can happen in a backyard, in a woodland temple, on the balcony of your high-rise apartment. Feed them (I give mine milk, corn liquor, cheap bright candy), honor them, talk to them. And it's best to do this when you aren't in a crisis so that they know you. It is always a good idea to build a relationship before you go asking for favors, don't you think? Ask the spirit of that maple tree or that rock or that hill to be with you in your hour of need. Ask them to guide and inspire you, to support you and to be your friend on the other plane.

Then come inside and, if you are a theist, clean off your home altar, the primary one. Dust the table, put on a clean cloth, make an effort to set up this beautiful focal point, this place between the worlds where you will petition the Divines. Burn some incense, add some flowers, whatever you do to make it fresh. My advice is to work directly with your own Divines, the ones you honor all the time. If you are dedicated to Artemis, ask Her to stand with you, to show you what you need to see. You don't need to go to Brigid for healing if you don't have a relationship with Her. Go first to your matrons and patrons, tell them the story, ask for help, ask for blessings.

Next, set up an Ancestor altar and actively engage your Ancestors. Your actual Ancestors—your mom or great-uncle or your older sister who died when you were ten. Feed them, honor them, and be very clear about how important they are to you and how much you need their help.

Now look at your life—what do you need? To banish something? To call something to you? Do you need to stand under a full moon and say the most important prayer—*thank you*? If you need to create a ritual of thanksgiving, then do it. Make it pure and simple. Get a babysitter if you need to. Fling yourself before your altar if that feels right.

Does your need require a spell? Then do one. Don't spend days researching the books of spells or Googling your request. Just do it. Make it up as you go along. Check the phase of the moon, and out of your need and your love, create a spell and do it. Raise a circle of pure energy and do it.

Do all those things, and do them all again if need be. Clarify your need and request for yourself and for your helpers both seen and unseen. And if nothing changes, consult an astrologer, get a tarot or rune reading, and try to figure out why this is happening to you now. Why again? Is there a lesson you need to be heeding? Are you facing the same challenges again and again? Why? What lesson are you not learning? And why not?

Many books have been written about daily spiritual practice, most of it from the Christian traditions. When tragedy—or merely drama—strikes, they have recourse to heavy-duty praying, just as we do. But if they—and we—have cultivated a clear series of steps to get grounded and feel our connection to the Divines, it can make those scary times a little less stressful.

Start the morning by grounding yourself and finish your day by looking at the moon and saying your prayers. There is comfort there and connection.

CHAPTER SIX

FLAMES OF LONGING AND DESPAIR

I conjure here a circle of power, a shield against evil, a boundary between the worlds of Earth and ether, a rampart and protection that shall preserve and contain the power that we shall raise within. I bless and consecrate this circle, in the name of the Elder Ones.

Several years ago, the Alewives discovered something strange in the act of grounding (which we discussed in Chapter Three). We dutifully sent the tiny energy roots through the bottoms of our feet and into the bosom of the planet, as I usually name it. Growing stronger as they descended, those roots brought us to a place of oneness, a place that felt strong and safe and secure.

And then we felt a sort of ripple, a swift jerk below the surface. It brought with it a sense of impermanence and liquidity. We stood upon, not our sturdy reliable planet, but something more malleable. Something frightening, anxiety provoking. If the Earth itself is not solid, what can be relied on?

We can. All of us. When we learn to work across all the artificial boundaries, we can rely on each other and our profound human connection. But that is not our current skill, whether in the vast wasteland of social media or face-to-face. We live in a time when we are best at judging each other's every action, checking against our subtle lists of virtues to make sure we can tick every box. And if not, we are obligated to call out the miscreants, whoever they are, whatever they are. In Chapter Eleven, we will return to the layers of culture and habit that threaten our struggle for resilience: the creation of those circles on the ground that may (or may not) be part of the scheme for our species' survival.

For now, we will explore the importance and protocols for shielding ourselves so that our work in these Tower Times can proceed with as little interference as possible.

Shielding is the act of putting energetic panels around your person to protect you from free-ranging energy pulses that can disturb your personal field.

What it means in regular terms is that if you are feeling unbalanced and out of sorts and there's no apparent reason, you can utilize this technique to help you get your balance back, to aid in your discernment process. In addition to grounding (which we've covered), shielding helps you ward off those free roamers that might be contributing to your lack of focus or ease.

It's a wonderful coping mechanism. In these terribly distracting times, it is often hard to focus on our priorities, and these simple techniques of relaxation, grounding, and shielding are invaluable. Working collectively with colleagues and friends can sometimes require the skills of a diplomat instead of the sharpness and belligerence of a warrior.

For example, I was in a long and fraught meeting recently. Not tedious so much as unsettling, an endurance trial. It got very interesting though when it seemed as if one of my colleagues was attacking me. Not physically, of course, but I began to get very prickly. My own irritation was heightened, and I could feel myself preparing for a verbal battle to squash my opponent.

But then I remembered that my colleague was in a delicate place emotionally and was, even at the best, prone to being a little harsh in judgment. So I dug my heels into the carpet and grounded myself—something

I've suggested to clients and friends more times than I can count. I pulled energy up through the Earth and brought all that lovely energy into my belly button and took some deep breaths. Then I set some shields. It's just like *Star Trek*, as I remind my classes. If you feel attacked, before returning tit for tat, say to yourself—shields up—and then do it. Breathe deeply. Look around you. Count to ten if that is a usable tactic for you.

With the technique I prefer, it's exactly like casting a circle. The shield is broad and curved so that when you've raised up four of them, they make a glittery curved wall around you. I start in the North and raise before me a shield of emerald. When I feel that solidly and can imagine the greenness of it, I set a shield of diamond at my right hand, a shield of ruby behind me and a shield of sapphire to my left. I see them joined at the edges and solid. I take another deep breath and imagine the panels then flow under the surface of the land to form a bowl under my feet. The shielding is complete as it creates an arch above my head to form a sort of umbrella.

It should happen very quickly, once you practice and get the knack for it. I also imagine that the shields make a clanging sound as they rise into place. Not logical, of course, because gemstones don't clang. But it always makes me think of those metal doors at banks and malls. Safe as houses.

Some people actually are under energetic attack (psychic attack) from other people, but mostly it's sensitive people like yourselves who are catching the energies that are flowing through the universe and over the face of our dear old Earth.

When they get to be too much or when their activity catches you at a vulnerable time—shields up!

Though I am currently on sabbatical, I have done a fair amount of interfaith work. I am still on email lists and in Facebook groups that joyfully announce the holy day of a minority religion so that we all feel better about "other people's" religions. I often dream of interfaith engagement going past our commonalities to reasonably discuss our real differences. I am still waiting for that group.

Several years ago, I was sent a letter from interfaith powerhouse and legitimately good thinker, Rabbi Michael Lerner. His work on the transformative healing of the world through the power of divine love is called Tikkun Olam, and his commitment to that work is humbling.

Except when it is annoying. In the letter, Rabbi Lerner hit all the right notes for the sort of multifaith work that is so popular in the West, but he had to get in a dig at Burning Man. Don't get me wrong—I will never attend Burning Man because I am a pasty woman who can't easily tolerate temperatures above eighty-five and is happiest in the damp coolness of a Scottish spring.

But his implication was that the event was problematic and required a "spiritual" alternative. So I wrote to him.

Good morning, Rabbi Lerner!

A dear friend of mine in the United Religions Initiative forwarded me a recent email from you, concerning a letter from clergy to Senator Obama. I am involved in a young interfaith group, and she thought to network the letter to more progressives and independent thinkers among the clergy.

I was intrigued and a little saddened by this paragraph, an addendum to your initial note—

"Would you be interested in working with me to help create a week-long interfaith encampment for the summer... aimed at people ages 20-40 as a spiritual alternative to Burning Man (the annual event in

November that draws 40-50,000 young people—check it out by Googling it, and if you don't know how to do that, well, you aren't the right person to help us build this event). Our gathering would be a celebration of spiritual progressives whose commitment to God, Spirit, or Love brings them into or sustains their work in Tikkun Olam (the healing and transformation of the world)."

I certainly understand wanting to put together an interfaith encampment. In my spiritual community (I am an Earth Religionist and a Wiccan), we love to come together outdoors, to create a time outside time and a place between the worlds. You are mistaken if you think Burning Man is not a celebratory and spiritual gathering of the tribes. Frankly, I am too old and pale for a week in the desert, but there are official and unofficial "burns" all over the country. We recently had one here in the mountains of NC called "Transformus."

These events bring together many kinds of people, and some of them may seem more prone to party than to pray, but Burning Man is one of those places between the worlds that is transformative, ecstatic, joyful, and peaceful. It draws people who choose an intense exploration of their spirituality, with people of like mind. Often their goal is personal—and thereby global—transformation. They live in harmony with each other and the Earth, and they create a place where authority is not hierarchical and top down but flows from the microvillages of the tribal gathering.

They are harkening back to an ancient form of worship and to the shamanic work that is done in countless cultures across this dear old world. By all means, create an interfaith encampment—a gathering of the tribes—that enforces and sustains healing of the planet. But don't place it in opposition to another beloved and intensely spiritual event. Burning Man is not vacation Bible school, and thank goodness for that!

I never heard back from him, which didn't surprise me in the least. But I hope he took a moment from his busy schedule to consider that not everyone gathered around a bonfire is singing "Kumbaya."

We are in strange and troubling times now, and calling it Tower Time and constantly forcing you to remember what is arguably the most dramatic card in the tarot really isn't helping, is it? Good. Supermoons keep popping up. People on Facebook somehow never manage to know when the planet Mercury is retrograde, even though it distresses and affects them in some mighty ways. Eclipses go from fascinating celestial observation to spiritual danger zone and are very powerful times in the world of Pagans and magic workers. For one thing, it's a full moon. A time of pregnant power and also a kind of stasis before the moon begins to wane. Add into that effect the darkening of the moon—the shadow of the dear old Earth made visible on the shining face of the moon. It is as if the universe is bent on showing us our weaknesses and giving us a chance to practice calling in the resources we need.

Letting Go of Fear

That biblical admonition frequently flows through my fingers and into the ether—fear not. Fear not! For behold! Some fear is necessary because humans aren't nearly as observant and dangerous as we wish we were or cosplay that we are. For those unreasonable fears, though, we can engage processes that will help us override the flight/fight/freeze reaction that is hardwired into the species. We can name our fear, refusing to travel with its heavy and annoying burden.

Try this. Hold a flat glass marble in your nondominant hand and speak your fear aloud. Tap the glass marble with the middle finger of your dominant hand, setting the intention. Send the fear—a very specific fear—into the small glass marble—holding the tips of your fingers on it as you breathe and ground. When the energy is released, break contact with the marble. Place it in running water or bury it in the yard.

I leave you now with this benediction, these "good words."

We are the keepers of the flame. As we stand here, we also look for lights that proclaim freedom and hope, passion and warmth. The flame is the central symbol in many of the world's faith traditions—a flame that is the light of freedom and truth—and within the halo of its glowing is the place where peace can be waged, justice served, and community built.

We are the keepers of the flame. We leave this holy place knowing that we travel forth as kindred spirits, bound by our love and respect for each other. The flame we hold today in honor in our hearts will bring clarity, and we will carry it still, each to each, in brightness and trust and love. Be the light, dear friends. May you always keep the flame. Blessed be.

CHAPTER SEVEN

FIRST LOVE: WATER

"And through this distemperature we see
The seasons alter: hoary-headed frosts
Fall in the fresh lap of the crimson rose,
And on old Hiems' thin and icy crown
An odorous chaplet of sweet summer buds
Is, as in mockery, set: the spring, the summer,
The childing autumn, angry winter change
Their wonted liveries, and the mazed world,
By their increase, now knows not which is which."
—William Shakespeare, *A Midsummer Night's Dream*

As you grow more confident in your ritual-making abilities, you can play with the elements of ritual, finding new ways to honor the elements that make up ourselves and our world. Following an extraordinary flood in the high country where I live, a group of people came together to mourn the losses and to honor the power of living water.

We sat together in a circle and spoke of our immediate experiences with the racing waters. One of the rivers that flooded was called Tahkeeostee by the indigenous Tsalagi/Cherokee, and that name means "racing waters." Now it is called the French Broad, and it flows two hundred and ten miles through the hills of western North Carolina and into the hills of eastern Tennessee, joining the Holston to become the Tennessee River near Knoxville.

This cast is specific to our area. Feel free to adapt it to your needs.

Circle Cast: The Waters

North: Sweet, sweet water for our own drinking—deep in a rough gourd—and for the nourishment of tree and fox and beetle. Quiet, but for tree frogs and crows calling, left peaceful for our constant need. We honor the great reservoir of blue waters in Bee Tree Lake and the North Fork!

East: Mother of waters, wet road of our Ancestors. We play on the hot sands at Edisto and search for perfect shells, careful to leave the turtle mothers to their egg laying. We stand in awe of your strong winds in Frances, Ivan, and Jeanne. We honor the constant movement of salty water in the far Atlantic Ocean!

South: Bed for kayaks, friendly neighbors, we watch you from the asphalt roads. You are tame, domesticated, backdrop to our play and work. But then you heaved up, rolling over and through us, silting pathways, tossing tree trunks. The rivers remind us, and we honor the power of our neighbors, the Swannanoa and the French Broad, called Tahkeeostee!

West: Slow and wide, the river called Old Man fans out into the Gulf. He carries commerce, he carries happy travelers, and sand. Splitting the continent with brown water, splitting east from west, flowing out of the north and into the sun. We honor the cleft of wide, deep Mississippi!

In A Rough Gourd: a Sonnet of Water

After a frightening flood on the French Broad and Swannanoa rivers, several of us came together to do a ritual to bring healing to the swollen waters and drowned land. The ritual honored the strength and beauty of the waters and acknowledged our great debt to their presence. We began the ceremony by casting an intentional circle. A circle cast usually honors four elements, as associated with four directions. But our cast was designed to keep us mindful of the water that surrounds us here in the mountains of western North Carolina. So we celebrated in a circle in which each direction was water.

We know that Earth is mostly water as we ourselves are mostly water. When the rains come too often, the floods are awesome, as well as awful. When the rains refuse to come, the land lies parched and the fear of lost food crops and lost power consumes us.

I grew up in a cove in western Buncombe County in the middle parts of the last century. Because we lived at the head of the cove, the water in the city lines often didn't make it to our house. My father had built a concrete-block reservoir when my parents first moved to the house, and that worked for a few years.

But when my brother and I were born, my mother was afraid the reservoir would be a too-tempting hazard and had my father knock a hole in the eastern wall. So water became a commodity for us as I was growing up, a sometimes doubtful commodity.

We didn't have an indoor bathroom, so our water usage was confined to washing clothes, dishes and bodies, and to cooking. The summer sometimes saw us without water because the drain on the system increased with gardens and car washing nearer the water's source. And because the pipes weren't buried deeply, we were often waterless in winter when the supply pipes froze.

We would bring water from a spring near my cousin's house, hauling it along the dirt road in plastic milk jugs and large cooking pots. I loved that spring, which had been domesticated many years before with a beautiful stone facing. We knelt on the flat stones in the front, opened a wooden door with screen wire in it, and dipped into the sharp cold of a mountain spring. The water was sweet, and I don't remember it ever running dry.

There was a freshwater stream that ran through our property, and it, like the city water, ran wet and dry, depending on the season. My brother and I used to dam it up with stones and sticks and catch salamanders and crawdads in the small pools.

For me there has always been a sacred element to water. Partly astrological (I'm a Pisces with moon in Scorpio) and partly due to its scarcity in my upbringing, my love and reverence for water have never wavered down the long road of the years since then. Now I live in the city, and there is a rush of water from the tap and a flush of water in the toilet. There are great barrels under the eaves of the house that supply the water for houseplants and garden.

But one of my greatest pleasures is to play in the water from the downspout, where it pools up on the east side of the house. I use a large clamshell and move it from place to place, wishing only for salamanders in the coolness of it.

And always wondering if there will be enough for all that we ask water to do.

Here in the southern mountains of Appalachia, the people still cling—at least some of us do—to the old elements that ensure the continuation of the species— dirt, sun, water, and good luck. All in exactly the right proportions, except the luck, of which we will take as much as we can get. These elements link us across cultures and through time, welding us together in a circle as strong as steel. We feel that circle bending now, fraying like old ribbon, as we face the threats of overdevelopment and careless land use.

Let's look at the historical relationship of traditional mountain people to this necessary ingredient of life and also explore the current trends in water use and management that threaten this relationship.

There are springs and headwaters in these mountains that feed into the great rivers of the American southeast, and these secret areas were protected in the days of the Woodland-era peoples, in the time of the Cherokee and even in the early days of white settlement. It was deemed necessary to keep the flow of water pure, and the placing of cow pasture and outhouse was done in relation to the spring or creek. From our Ancestors in the British Isles we brought a reverence for water that expressed itself in "dressing" the wells of Britain and Ireland in bright wreaths of herbs and flowers.

The religious sensibilities of the earliest residents were reshaped with the coming of western Christianity to the mountains. But the sanctity of water that brings traditional Cherokee to the rivers, "to the water," is also seen in the small mountain churches that have a painting of the river Jordan over the baptismal pool beyond the altar. The full immersion of the believer in a body of running water marks an important passage in Christian belief and ceremony. To feel oneself made clean in the water was—for both the Cherokee and the European settlers—an act of spiritual purification and a place of healing.

The area also attracts spiritual seekers and pilgrims who come from an Earth-centered spiritual perspective. Through their invocation of the four classical elements of earth, air, fire, and water, the celebration of water comes full circle to a place of spiritual prominence.

From ancient, pre-Contact times, many springs were imbued with a spirit or spirits that gave the waters special powers. There is a cove in west Buncombe County which boasts of such a spring—a drink that is said to bring fertility to any woman of childbearing years who partakes of it. There's a spring in Madison County that is said to bring healing to anyone suffering from headaches or back pain. Such springs were once treasured as literal fountains of healing, but with the coming of modern medicines, their curative powers were forgotten or unneeded.

As we bring modern holistic approaches in healing to the traditional ethnobotany of this region, we again turn to the old ways of "yarb" gathering (whether ginseng or bloodroot), and we recall those old springs with their curative powers. But the bond between the people who lived directly from the land and the places they called home began to break when mountain folks left the coves and hollers to pursue work in urban areas, whether in mill or factory. Unable to make a living from the land, the children of farming families chose to leave the land in search of a gentler life.

This vital element—important to all life and indeed the matrix of all life on the planet—has become a political issue in many places on the planet, and the southeastern US is no exception. Due to the drought conditions leading up to the devastation of 2007, several state governments (notably those of Georgia, Alabama, and Tennessee) are casting about for the legal definition of who owns the water.

The last decade has seen a drastic change in the topography and demographics of the mountain region. Highly desirable as a tourist and retirement destination, people are drawn here from all over the US. The development on the steep slopes of the mountain—the houses that are sited not for arable land but for the "viewshed"—put a particular strain on the waters. The Land of Sky Regional Council commissioned a study of steep slope development, and the impact on water is staggering. Construction runoff, silting of streams, even overuse of wells in those deeply rural areas cause concern for the quality as well as quantity of water regionally.

As our understanding of the basics of good health grow to encompass not only the quality of the water we drink but also the distance that water must come, we are all made aware of the importance of this simplest of chemical compounds. In an age when we may imbibe water from France or Fiji, it makes sense to seek our own local sources of water, to protect and appreciate them as the oldest residents of this old land did. We must do this for the health of the land and all of us who depend on it.

A Personal and Private Self-Blessing Ritual to Start the Day

Place your palms flat on the top of your head and take three deep breaths. Say aloud or to yourself: I am blessed with the blessing of the land around me, of my Ancestors and of the Divines. I am here and strong, and my heart is open.

And you can repeat that at any time during your day when you feel alone or stressed or anxious. You are so blessed, at all times.

CHAPTER EIGHT

WALKING BETWEEN THE WORLDS OF EARTH

A damsel with a dulcimer
In a vision once I saw:
It was an Abyssinian maid,
And on her dulcimer she played,
Singing of Mount Abora.
Could I revive within me
Her symphony and song,
To such a deep delight 'twould win me,
That with music loud and long,
I would build that dome in air,
That sunny dome! those caves of ice!
And all who heard should see them there,
And all should cry, Beware! Beware!
His flashing eyes, his floating hair!
Weave a circle round him thrice,
And close your eyes with holy dread,
For he on honey-dew hath fed,
And drunk the milk of Paradise.

—Samuel Taylor Coleridge, Excerpted from "Kubla Khan"

This is the chapter in which we consider moving between the worlds of matter and spirit as a corrective to Tower Time and as a way to get more information. We will also look at the Baba Yaga and her sudden appearance in the mountains of western North Carolina.

As we begin to unpack our nonmaterial experiences in community and through social media, more people are coming forward to talk about that odd dream they had or the unusual daydreams that come to them unaware. I think of those people—and I am one of them—as intuitive shamans. And here is the place I need to define—if not that word—at least the functions of that position in society.

I have always been told that the word shaman is specific to a particular culture, and as a result I often say a "shamanic practitioner," which is awkward. I know people who are Michael Harner-trained shamanic practitioners, people who follow an indigenous tradition for this work, and many years ago I met an Inuk man named Angaangaq, who called himself a shaman, sang into his rubber-headed frame drum, and taught me to do the same.

The words used to describe this practice are many and varied. Some are loaded with history. Others are loaded with attitude. The practices are completely cross-cultural and surprisingly similar from place to place. Our working definition of the practice is to facilitate a wide range of healing through interaction with the nonmaterial spirit world. A person who follows these ancient traditions is a walker between the worlds of matter and spirit.

Some of you may find that another way to gather information to get through these challenging times is to do this sort of engagement with the nonphysical world. If this work calls to you, you can get training in a variety of places, or you can do it intuitively, as I seem to have done.

Personally, I have only had on-the-job training in these techniques. In many cases, I haven't consciously chosen to do this spirit walking but have done it out of desperation or completely accidentally. As I feel the burden of these changing times and the concerns of my local community, I am engaging in these intuitive shamanic practices more often and feel I'm getting more adept in the utilization.

For years I could get to trance through dance and drinking alcohol. Recently I joined a group with the intention of learning how to reach a trance state more quickly and with less rum. I've been trying different things to get to that deep and watchful state, and I share them here for your information and not as the be-all and end-all of how this should be done.

Going to the Akashic Record

Many people find it easy to travel in their dreams, and I am no exception. Having been a frequent visitor to bookshops and a bookseller myself for many years, I dream sometimes of going into a particular book store. It is always the same bookshop, and I came to know that it was a storehouse of information. It was the legendary repository of the so-called "akashic record."

Here's what it looks like and how I get there. I'm in a shopping mall that is curiously empty. Sometimes I ride down an escalator and sometimes walk down a wide corridor, and I come to a bookshop whose doorway is in a corner, like an old-fashioned drugstore. There are three steps down, and they and the rest of the shop are covered in a deep-piled moss-green carpet.

The place is very quiet and has that bookstore smell that all book lovers know and appreciate. There are other people in the store, but we don't interact much. We nod and smile at each other but tend to go our own way.

Long wooden tables—like bars in Western movies— are set at intervals throughout the shop. I walk up to an empty one and put my hand flat down on the smooth, cool surface. A book slides down the length of the table, and I open it up and begin to read, using my finger to run along the lines.

Flying Upright and Dining with the Icicle People

The trance group afforded me the following experience. A good friend has an autoimmune disease that is confusing and hard to both treat and diagnose. I told her I would journey for her and see what came of it, making no promises that she would see results. Our group works with various trance-inducing postures, and I chose to lie on my side on a sheepskin, à la the Sleeping Priestess of Malta. Eyes closed, I listened to a CD of drumming and began with a vision I had used before.

I am standing alone on a clean, pebbly beach, and the tide has gone out beyond the horizon. I rise from the balls of my feet and fly, standing upright. I fly to the Alps and walk past a glacier up and up. At the top of the mountain, I watch signal fires light across the hills, starting from left to right. I turn to the right and walk up a set of stone steps and come to a place where a circle of people dressed in furs and leather or moss and icicles sit around a fire. They welcome me with a shout, and I sit. We pass around a big pot of stew, eating it by pulling off pieces of what looks like corn pone and scooping out chunks of meat and juices. The pot goes around and around the circle, and the talk and laughter continue. It is time to leave, and I wipe my right hand on my thigh, cleaning the stew off it. I go to the edge of the cliff, and I fly away, the same as before, standing upright.

I come to a northern forest of deciduous trees and firs. I land standing upright, and there is a large badger there with a piece of folded paper under his left paw. I was thinking of how to get the paper— Do I ask for it? Will the badger give it? Then a peahen pokes her head up from behind a log and starts feeding the badger by putting bits of food into the side of the badger's mouth with her beak. The two of them leave, going in opposite directions. The badger leaves the paper, and I pick it up. I watch them walk away and say out loud, "I can't read this." A voice at my shoulder—I think it was the Morrighan (which is another story for another day)—said, "It's not for you." I take the paper with me and fly in the same way back to the lone beach. Then it starts to rain.

ଠଃଓ

I live in a place where people want to know more about western mystery traditions and can attend a weekend workshop or retreat that won't cost a lot of money.

Not too long ago, I sat in an auditorium with a large group of well-meaning and mostly white people who smelled nice and had warm coats. We were singing about and talking about and dancing about peace. I do that a lot. Those groups of gentle people wish desperately that the world was a better place and have a vague notion of peace as the answer to all the world's ills. Some think you can't have peace without justice. Some quote King and Gandhi. I will see those good people again in January when we all participate in the annual M. L. King peace march downtown, which will culminate in prayers to gods I don't honor and boring speeches that are difficult to hear outdoors. The war we've sown in the land between the mighty Tigris and the beautiful Euphrates continues to bear dark fruits, and my email inbox sees a new invitation to protest in the town square at least once a week. An overdue drink with an old friend can only be scheduled after she's finished standing silently in black, round and sullen as an old Greek widow.

Engagement, protest, focus. Material worlds intersecting the spiritual ones.

My email inbox is the frequent recipient of outraged and sorrowing emails about the state of Stonehenge in England and the Hill of Tara in Ireland. Both places have been important cultural markers in my personal spiritual journey, and I have been awed and privileged to spend time at each monument. Both are endangered, say the emails from friends and colleagues, by the coming of new development. A new road is being cut through the valley near Tara, and the historically important plains around the Great Henge will soon host a giant Tesco warehouse. It feels to many people as though it is a desecration of the sacred landscape that is vital to the cultural identity of those two places and to the spiritual identity of modern Pagans all over the world.

I've been thinking about the landscape lately. How could I not? Every time I turn around, someone is stripping the trees off a section of fragile hillside and planting a cluster of goofy-looking structures on it. As much as I love Tara and Wiltshire, my sacred landscape is here in the mountains that hold my Ancestors' bones and ashes. I've watched the changes of the past decades, and some of them fit the pattern of change in the area. I feel sure every generation that witnesses and pays for the change gripes and grumbles. There were "White Only" bathrooms underground in the town square in the 1970s—losing those was a vast improvement. But the multistory cracker-box buildings? The big-box stores and faux-Victorian MacMansions? That is a matter of opinion, of taste, of history in the landscape.

Natives talk about where our granddads bought horse feed and our aunties picked blueberries. We're insufferable that way—what must the newcomers think, those people who have no roots and don't care to have any? My roots make my head spin sometimes, make my back ache with the loss and the turmoil. The new developments that creep down the slopes are the least of my worries. There are whole blocks and opera houses and grand hotels that have been lost in this place. In every place, as change comes from the outside, bringing coveted jobs and arrogant incomers.

Lately I've taken to blaming it all on the Baba Yaga. Baba Yaga comes out of the Eastern European folk tradition, and she flies through the air in a mortar, using the pestle as a rudder. In fairy tales, she is a hag who is mostly avoided but occasionally sought out for her expert advice. She is opinionated and inscrutable, as all older women are, and she can't be relied upon to behave as she should. I have given a mountain spin to her name and think of her here in my hills as Granny Yaga.

It is somewhat bad form for one witch to blame another, but I've noticed that her houses have sprung up in my community, and that is a sure sign she is in residence. As more and more people move to this area, looking for Nirvana, there is no more flat land upon which to build. The shoulders of the mountains themselves must now bear the burden of the nouveau riche looking for vacation mountain homes. The new houses perch on steel posts, jutting out from the bare and rolling slopes.

Out-of-town developers have grown a line of Baba Yaga houses, silhouetted against the evening sky, and they strike terror into the heart of anyone who sees them. They are perched on their chicken legs, high on the bank. Houses that defy gravity, the wind whistling around their steel supports—how do you insulate such a place? Who lives in a Baba Yaga house on chicken legs, and how much have they paid? How much do we pay for the systematic destruction of our sacred landscape, and once we have lost that ineffable spirit, we can't regain it or return to it. Once lost, it will take more than the Baba Yaga to bring back the feeling of home and place that is easy to sense but hard to define.

We don't talk much about the spiritual dimensions of our communities, unless we are talking about specific spiritual communities. In tribal times, all of Earth was spirited, peopled with spirits indigenous to a place or a spring or an outcropping of stone. That spiritual energy seems confined now to "places of worship," which may be one of the results of the monotheists that conquered most of the known world. They strove to contain the powers of the unseen inside designated structures. We are fortunate indeed that those powers can't be managed or contained for long.

There are still some places in the world where the country folk will talk about how a certain area is peopled by ghosts or little people, but the larger culture has mostly lost the notion of a place having a soul. With the reemergence of Earth religions, however, we are seeing the intentional re-sacralizing of the landscape.

I have resolved to take it up with that Wise Woman of the Woods, our Granny Yaga, and to remember that one only approaches her if the need is great. The approach must be carefully planned, one's intention pure, and it's always wise to practice unfailing good manners.

Just like you'd approach your grandma.

CRES

Endehuanna's hymns to Inanna are among the oldest written prayers in the world (c. 3500-1900 BCE). Inanna is a Sumerian divinity, a Goddess of war and love, among other things. The body of Her liturgical cycle includes Her descent into the world of the dead to meet with Her sister Erishkegal, who reigns there.

It is a profound mythic cycle, and my religious work has included this as a meditation for several decades. I share it here for a couple of reasons. As we deeply engage the passages of these Tower Times, there will be occasions when you must—for your own sanity—retreat to a solitary state while continuing to do your work. You can choose to do this meditative journey alone, quietly, for as long or short a time as you need.

Our collective work in these times is subject to all the human emotions and vagaries of the rest of our lives. One too many meetings, yet another nonsensical argument on a social media platform, or a flash-fire misunderstanding with your beloved can drive you inward to regroup and recharge. This meditation works in those incidents to keep you connected with the work while doing the healthy thing and disconnecting for a while from your community. As I wrote in Going to Ground in Tower Time, we sometimes need a self-imposed timeout to continue to have the strength and outlook necessary for this endurance trial.

You may find taking private personal time to be helpful as a spiritually enhancing practice, one that you schedule for yourself on a regular or semiregular basis. The four Quarter days that are the solstices and equinoxes are good times to go inward, recalibrate, and return.

Whatever way you choose to use it (if you choose to do so), the Descent of Inanna is a powerful reset in a confusing world. I suggest you record it at a slow pace so that you can listen instead of reading. You may choose to use props that mimic the ones mentioned in the original text. They are listed at each gate below.

A Personal Meditative Ritual: The Descent of Inanna

The Great Below and Its Gates—a Journey Through the Dark-Facing Passageways (c. 3500-1900 BCE).

From the Great Above
she opened her ear to the Great Below
From the Great Above
the Goddess opened her ear to the Great Below
From the Great Above
Inanna opened her ear to the Great Below
—Wolkstein and Kramer, 52

This is a meditation. All that occurs within it happens in your mind's eye. You may choose to have props, if that helps you to feel a part of the world your mind and spirit are creating.

Approaching the Inner World

You stand on the edge of a great plain. Mountains lie in the distance, and the city sets behind you. You are clothed in your sacred garments and carry with you the accoutrements of your life journey. Regulate your breathing now, making it slow and even. Spend several minutes relaxing into this breathing, feeling your heartbeat slow as the energy of the world around you settles.

When you are ready, bend your knees slightly and focus your attention on the hills. You are Inanna, and this trial is one of your choosing. It is not imposed on you.

With your focus on the hills, you begin to run toward them across the great plain. This part of the meditation is to free you from the constraint of your

literal surroundings and to further move you into the
place of the myth, as well as the mystery. Run for as long
or short a time as feels right for your intention.

Breathe. You arrive at last at the doorway that opens
into the inner world. You are not breathless. Your heart is
strong. Your intention is clear. With your accoutrements
and garments around you, you approach the gatekeeper.
(In the myth, the gatekeeper's name is Neti.)

The gatekeeper demands your name. Think on that
for a moment. How will you enter this land from which
none return? Your given name? A chosen name? The
name you choose may change each time you do this
meditation. (In the myth, Inanna answers, I am Inanna,
Queen of Heaven.)

The gatekeeper leaves you now, turning swiftly away
to confer with his mistress Erishkegal. When this inner
queen is given the information that you have arrived,
she is not pleased and orders all the gates closed against
you. The gatekeeper relays this to you as you stand in the
doorway.

Breathe. You are denied an easy entry, an entry that
befits who you are. This is the first challenge. How will
you achieve your intention when you are so completely
blocked? Do you turn back, defeated? Sit with defeat
and frustration. Feel the effects of it on your physical
body. Have your shoulders tightened? Is your breathing
shallower? Attend to any changes and return yourself to
the moment you arrived at the mountains.

The gatekeeper has departed, leaving this doorway
unattended. Let your curiosity pull you forward to look
into the cool darkness.

You are facing the first gate. You realize you have
brought with you all you need to descend. At each gate,
you will make an offering of one of the tools you have
brought for the journey.

Gate One: the Turban

You remove the turban, which symbolizes your physical body (health, sexuality, life-force, chi).

Sit with that. Who are you without your personal energy and that energy that animates you? What gives you life?

When you are ready, proceed to the next gate.

Gate Two: the Necklace of Small Lapis Beads

You remove the necklace, which symbolizes the intellectual body (wisdom, acquired knowledge and its relationship to gnosis, including unverifiable personal gnosis/UPG).

Who are you without the accumulated knowledge and wisdom of your years? What are some of the things you "know" that you actually don't?

When you are ready, proceed to the next gate.

Gate Three: the Egg-shaped Beads at Her Breast

You offer up the egg-shaped beads, which symbolize the community body (creating, birthing, sundering, tribal mandates).

The egg has long been the icon for birth and generative life. Without your creativity—however you express that—what are you? How does it feel to lose this outlet?

When you are ready, proceed to the next gate.

Gate Four: the Seductive Pectoral

You offer up the pectoral collar, which symbolizes the intuitive body (prophecy and seership).

You are advised to "trust your gut," to listen to the still, small voice of your intuition. How do you navigate with that internal knowing when you can no longer "see" what lies around you or ahead of you? Without your intuition, how vulnerable are you?

When you are ready, proceed to the next gate.

Gate Five: the Golden Ring

You offer up the golden ring, which symbolizes the emotional body (right uses of power and attachments).

Emotion? But I am a slave to my emotions! Drop the unhelpful emotional baggage that the culture, your personal history, and your family of origin have imposed on you. How often do you use emotional displays to control the people around you, and is that healthy for you? When do you use your emotional body as an excuse for neglect of others or self?

When you are ready, proceed to the next gate.

Gate Six: the Lapis Tools for Measurement.

You offer up your measuring tools, which symbolize the spirita sancta on the Earth plane (working with spirit allies here—Ancestors, land spirits).

You feel yourself surrounded by unseen beings, some helpful, some constraining and shaming. How do you function in a world where you must rely on your wits and on the relationships you have with the people around you? Do you reach out to try to understand the people around you with whom you disagree politically? Spiritually?

When you are ready, proceed to the next gate.

Gate Seven: the Pala Dress

You offer up the pala dress (which may be that tiered and fringed skirt we see in the ancient images from this time), your final garment, which symbolizes the spirita sancta between the worlds (beyond time and matter; working with ancient memory, healing, remembering).

If you are someone who is working toward intentional goals, who dreams the future, how do you walk in the world without the expectation of that future time? How can you function, if you choose to, without an expectation of positive change or even reward for a job well done?

You have achieved the deepest level, and you have arrived unburdened by all the baggage that makes you you. Your wits, your great heart, and your offerings have gotten you to this point.

Your deepest self awaits you here—your shadow sister, your Erishkegal. She holds power over you because you have chosen to set aside your powers to enter into a relationship with your deepest self. You no longer get to fool yourself about who you are and who you can be.

Breathe. Breathe. Cross this space between you and go sit with her. With each step you will honor this deep self, and as you step closer to her, you begin to integrate her wisdom with yours. You come to sit beside her in her wide chair. Sit quietly there, coming into relationship with this deep you.

Take as much time here as you need. You may review recent disappointments or consider actions that have impacted you. You may find yourself simply sitting there, empty of all the things you have carried to exhaustion.

Rest, regroup. Here there is nourishment and nurturing. In this place there is healing, grace, and a kind of redemption. Let those flow over and through you, embracing you and your work. Let go of anything that you have managed to sneak past the gates, anything that no longer serves you.

When you are ready, feel yourself alone in the chair, refreshed and ready to return. Breathe. Connect with your heartbeat. Remember your name.

From the Great Below to the Great Above

Now we return to the plain above us, stretching out from that doorway in the mountains. We will gather up all the tools deposited at each gate. And with the reacquisition, we take a few moments to see if the tool in question is needful and how our relationship to it has changed because of our time in the deep.

Rise now and find yourself striding with purpose toward the final gate, which for you is now the first one. Before engaging the energy of Gate Seven, it may be helpful for you to turn back to the empty chair and assure yourself that this is also your place now, a place to which you may return in need or at leisure. There is always wisdom in this downward-and-upward journey.

Gate Seven: the Pala Dress

You pick up the pala dress, your first garment, which symbolizes the spirita sancta between the worlds (beyond time and matter; working with ancient memory, healing, remembering). You wrap it around your body.

What of healing did you learn in the deep? Review it for yourself. Tuck this new information, these new techniques, into your pala.

When you are ready, step through the gate with gratitude and curiosity.

Gate Six: the Lapis Tools for Measurement

You pick up your tools, which symbolize the spirita sancta on the earth plane (working with spirit allies here—Ancestors, land spirits). You feel the weight of them in your hands, judging their value to you.

How have your wits been sharpened to walk without your unseen companions? As you invite them to return and feel their presence around you—Ancestors, guardians and all—can you express your thanks for their advice, guidance, and company?

When you are ready, step through the gate with gratitude and curiosity.

Gate Five: the Golden Ring

You glimpse the shine of the golden ring, which symbolizes the emotional body (right uses of power and attachments).

Pick it up and take a moment to look at it in the palm of your hand. It is shiny and fits perfectly. Which finger does it go on? When you choose the finger and slip it on, you are engaging your own power again. What is power to you? How will you use it differently than before? Do you believe that you have this authority in the world even when the ring is gone?

When you are ready, step through the gate with gratitude and curiosity.

Gate Four: the Seductive Pectoral

Your pectoral collar presents itself on an alabaster pedestal. Remember it symbolizes the intuitive body (prophecy and seership).

As the collar touches the bones of your neck, feel the return of your intuition, your gut knowledge. How have you navigated without? How have you fared as a vulnerable being in the deep of your world?

When you are ready, step through the gate with gratitude and curiosity.

Gate Three: the Egg-shaped Beads at Her Breast

The egg-shaped beads, which symbolize the community body (creating, birthing, sundering, tribal mandates), have been awaiting your return. You clip them to the front of your pala dress and admire the clear blue of their lapis surfaces.

This reestablishes your relationship with your creative self. Has this time in the deep given you inspiration for new work, for doing the work you love in new ways?

When you are ready, step through the gate with gratitude and curiosity.

Gate Two: the Necklace of Small Lapis Beads

The necklace is on the floor, in the corner. It is small, easily overlooked. Remembering that it symbolizes your intellectual body (acquired knowledge and its relationship to gnosis, including unverifiable personal gnosis/UPG and wisdom), clasp it around your neck. Small, cool, and perfect beads of knowledge—can you add to this string? What areas of interest tickled your fancy as you left your acquired wisdom behind? New or expanded areas of study may be the result of this time away.

When you are ready, step through the gate with gratitude and curiosity.

Gate One: the Turban

You have reached the final gate, the one that began
your journey to this strangely familiar place. Wrap the
turban securely around your head and feel yourself
reconnect with your physical body (health, sexuality,
life-force, chi).

Stretch yourself. Check your breathing, your
heartbeat. Lick your fingers and then wiggle your toes.
Return fully to your physical self, embracing all that
you've gathered on your ascent to the doorway.

You are now fully restored, bringing back to yourself
the pieces that were necessary to shed in your descent to
the deep. Take a moment here to review the gates and
what you acquired or set aside at each.

When you are ready, step through the gate with
gratitude and curiosity and approach the doorway. You
have been a long time in the shadowed world of this
meditation. You are about to step back into the world
of light and shadow. Take a moment to prepare yourself
for that. When you are ready, step out into the sunlight
of the plain.

You are almost done here. Only one more place to
explore—the great apple tree in the plain of Kulaba.

You can see it across the plain—a large, many-
branched tree, tall and wide. As before, monitor where
your breathing is and how your heart beats. Breathe
yourself into a place of readiness. Turn back to look at
the doorway. Place your hand on it. Then turn to face
the plain and sprint to the apple tree. Run for as long
or short a time as feels best to you. When you reach the
tree, you will see a simple sturdy seat there, waiting for
you.

Sit down. Roll your shoulders forward and then back.
Straighten your spine and put your feet flat on the soil

of the plain. Place your hands on the tops of your thighs, palms up.

Breathe.

This is your personal seat of power, the place of your sovereignty. You may come to sit here anytime, with or without the full meditation. When your work causes you anxiety, come to this place. When you feel inappropriately powerless and weak, come here under this apple tree and regain your power.

Breathe.

When you are fully ready, please return to the world of your work, this place where towers are recalibrating as they fall, where your great heart and clear vision are so needed.

CR&O

This meditation departs from the myth in some obvious ways. In the myth cycle, Erishkegal turns on her sister "the eye of death" and hangs Inanna's body from a meat hook. In the meditation, I only use this image when I am guiding it for others. It is far too strong an image to engage in if you are unfamiliar with the lore or uncertain about the process of this meditation.

For the purpose of simplifying the meditation, we walk from the below through our own strength of will. In the myth, Inanna is rescued by her companion Ninshibur, accompanied by two creatures who bear the food and water of life— the kurgarra and the galatur.

And the apple tree on the plain of Kulaba is where Inanna discovers the one person who is not mourning her death—her lover and consort Dumuzzi. In our meditation, this is the place where we step into our own sovereignty.

CHAPTER NINE

A MAN IN THE MOON: DISTRIBUTION AND USES OF POWER

This lanthorn doth the horned moon present;
Myself the man in the moon do seem to be.
All I have to say, is, to tell you that the lanthorn is the moon; I,
the man in the moon; this thorn-bush, my thorn-bush; and this
dog, my dog.
—William Shakespeare, Snarveling,
A Midsummer Night's Dream

I am the guardian of travelers at night.
I help illuminate the fortune-teller's sight.
Forever changing.
Forever just the same.
I am the one.
I am the Man in the Moon.
—Brian Henke, "The Man in the Moon"

I hope you won't think it is far too late in this book to bring up the uses of power, but I have found it more understandable to write about the basics and how-tos before attempting the whys and wherefores. To understand why we need ceremony—as well as permaculture and water catchment—it is helpful to look at the ways power is shifting in these transitional times.

When we talk about the history of these systems we call patriarchy, we see a hierarchical system for power distribution. Generally speaking, men have been on the top of that hill, and this has given them sets of skills appropriate for wielding power over other groups of people, the land, and resources. It has also given women (and other beings not on the top of the hill fort) skills appropriate for their station in the hierarchy. If we are indeed watching the dissolution of these systems, it is time for us to discover new ways of working with authority and with power.

We are longing for the culture to settle down, to not hear one more report of a policeman shooting a black man or a lone white gunman shooting up a movie theater or school. How much more are we likely to endure in the horrific weather patterns that are the visible by-product of global climate change, a problem about which our leaders meet periodically to promise things they simply can't or won't do? Do the mountains and people of Appalachia now have to endure fracking—after a century of extraction industries have stripped out the trees (twice), the coal seams, blasted the mountains away into the creeks and hollers below in strip-mining—which doesn't even offer the cold comfort of decent wages?

It may in fact be time for all of us to return to a sense of personal autonomy, of personal agency. When we stand in the face of those enormous things we can't seem to alter with either voting or goodwill, it is time for us to return to ourselves and turn to each other.

Take a deep breath, friends. Ground yourself into the bosom of the Earth. Now, from this place of strength and relative safety, open your heart to those in need of your goodness, your strength. Your blessing. Speak gentle words to those who need them… and kick the rear ends of those that need that too.

The world is aswirl with chaotic energy right now. We always have choices then, but the two obvious ones are ground and hold—or ride the chaos. What we do tends to be determined by how strong we feel at the moment.

Going to ground like a little furry critter is always a good option. Engaging the powers—speaking truth to power—is the work of determined and often desperate souls for whom justice seems an indistinct possibility.

In times of grief and fear and fury, it is sometimes a comfort to sit with our own past and with those of our forebears, to remember what life was like when we grew all the food we ate, had no control over how many children we would bear, were ruled by custom and culture that considered those hard lives to be of less value than the lives of our "betters." We find blessing in such communion, as our reflections on their lives bring us wisdom, strength, vision.

Sometimes what we are doing is kindling past the apathy of culture and life. Sometimes we are lighting signal fires to let the next generation know that we care about the world we are leaving to them. Sometimes fire is light, sometimes it is heat. In its wake there is renewed life. I always take nature as my teacher, and I think about forest fires—the terror, the destruction, and the aftermath of livid green. It is all a cycle, you know. The Great Cycle.

Creation/Destruction/Creation

My exploration of the homeliness we pondered in an earlier chapter continued yesterday with temple cleaning and tidying. It will continue tonight with a massive cooking binge. A longtime member of our community is homebound for a while as she heals, and tomorrow is the day to visit and bring food. My counter has small containers of all sorts that will soon hold yummy things. I'll try to be aware of healthy foods for her healing body. Though, to be honest, I do think there's a healing quality in macaroni and cheese, so there'll be some of that in there too.

That's homely—that flotilla of recyclable containers—so let's add in the magical piece of it too. With every stirring and with every burp of those lids, I will add a wish for wellness, a spell, if you will. I will speak a prayer for swift and enduring healing and a robust return of her life-force.

As we consider returning to our whole selves, of remembering the things that make us... well, that make us humans, I naturally will recommend that you get dirty, that you garden and hike and watch the world shift in its seasons as it changes color and temperature.

Like the daffodils that emerge too soon in late winter and return to bloom for St. Dafydd's Day in March, be stubborn. Bloom bright. Return through the jumble of your past and your present—and get to the roots of who you are and what you love and what you won't put up with for one more minute. Let's strive to be proactive and less reactive in these changing times of ours. As we return, reground, regroup, let's—each of us—simply say enough is enough.

My intuition is that the years ahead are going to be at least as challenging as those gone by—but we now have many more skills for dealing with challenges and are now (due to the stresses of the previous years) much more resilient. We'll waste less time lamenting what we can't repair and much more time fixing what we can. We've learned lots of valuable lessons in the past years—we've dabbled in speaking out, on loving deeply, on tending the beings that require our tender and good attention. We have spoken of self-care and even done a bit of that. We have realized that we are in Tower Time now, this big cultural shifting—it is not coming down the pike or waiting for us over the next hill. We live in times of great change that require us to be thoughtful, intentional, and fearless.

For a couple of years, I belonged to a feminist book club—a haven for thought and planning and a place of refuge during this Tower Time. During the weeks-long discussion of our first book—Gerda Lerner's The Creation of Patriarchy—I came up with the notion of Sacra Ephesia, a mythic place based on historic Ephesus. It became a fanciful destination for our thoughts about the time after patriarchy though we could barely manage to think of such a thing. An idea about egalitarian work divisions would begin with "in Sacra Ephesia..."

As you may or may not know, Ephesus was sacred to the Goddess Artemis. She was not only matron of the city but Her veneration was an important part of the urban economy. When Paul was writing to the "Ephesians," he was encouraging those beleaguered Christian missionaries who were working on the conversion of the populace for whom the Artemisian pilgrims were a sort of cash cow.

The purveyors of food, drink, accommodation, and religious tchotchkes didn't want to give Artemis up because She was good to them, one imagines, both spiritually and economically. Eventually they gave in—as so many cultures did—and accepted the new religion.

Our book club lamented the loss of the great library at Alexandria, but we worked on reinventing Ephesus as the seat of transitional power. We envisioned the sacred precinct—a place of safety and devotion. This Sacra Ephesia was also something that we could carry in our hearts and on our souls, as the times and the land around us grew more incomprehensible.

In winter, as the Wheel slowed to a standstill and the planting season felt so distant, we dreamed this beautiful place in the springtimes of our souls. We sat gazing back to what we know of Artemis's Ephesus, with its library, theater, and temples. And we also saw the imagined Ephesia of the future: not only a small historic stop on our vacation to beautiful Turkey but a place of peace and joy that each of us called our own and carried in our fertile imaginations.

Our own private Ephesus. Sacra Ephesia.

Holding a place of potential and optimism can be terribly important when we face such enormous and painful changes. If that place must live for now in our fantasies, it can still be a very useful metaphor.

೦೫೪

The following is a direct result of contemplating the possible role of this mythic and dream-laden place.

Here in Sacra Ephesia, we have had a glass of clean water as a morning ablution, and we drink it with joy and tremendous gratitude. We vow that today we will go out into the sunshine. We will stop and take three deep breaths—and listen for rain. May your day be powerful and rich... and very grounded. You are loved... and needed.

Here in Sacra Ephesia, we relish the sight of tiny bats, twisting their way across the crescent moon. We are mindful of so many things and yet... and yet... there must always be a moment of beauty in which to honor bats. Mustn't there?

Here in Sacra Ephesia, we are feeling the pull of the downward slide of the agricultural year. The insects are bright and joyful in their pillaging—tiny warlords of crop disaster. The soil speaks through a parched throat, and we must attend as priestesses of all that is holy: dirt, earthworms, mulch, food.

Here in Sacra Ephesia, it has been a long and winding weekend, dear friends. We can barely believe that we started the day standing in the mist of a holy circle and spent the end of the daytime touring a new parish hall. Ah, the smell of construction. Now it is time for the fruit of the vine.

The Moon and the Sun

A contemplation of our solar system's star and our planet's satellite turns my mind to Sol Invictus, and my appreciation for celebrations of the winter solstice grows.

The word solstice comes from the Latin sol stetis—sun stands still. Winter solstice is when, because of the tilt of our planet, our hemisphere is leaning farthest away from the sun, and therefore the daylight is the shortest and the sun has its lowest arc in the sky. Sounds simple, doesn't it? It's an astronomical occurrence that happens every year, more regularly than clockwork. And this time of growing light has been memorialized since before recorded history as the rebirth of the sun. Holy days abound this time of year—and Hallmark seems to be catching up with the notion that not everyone celebrates Christmas. There was even a display of Chanukah junk—plastic dreidels, potholders with a menorah pattern, an electrified channakeim where you screw in a light bulb each evening—at the local pharmacy. I can only imagine the joy of finding a similar display of plastic Yule logs, Mithras coffee mugs, and tiny golden tops that play "Here Comes the Sun" when spun, once this winter solstice thing really catches on.

Some people believe that, at their root, solstice celebrations grew out of an ancient fear that the failing light would never return unless humans intervened with anxious vigil or antic celebration. I'm not sure I buy that. There's a fair amount of recent scholarship on our Neolithic Ancestors, and I think we short-change them and ourselves when we think of them cowering in caves, frantically lighting greasy fires in hopes of placating the sun. Humans are natural observers, and the more natural the human the more dependent they are on their powers of observation. Neolithic peoples were the first farmers, after all. They would have been intimately tied to the cycles of the seasons in their biosphere because life is dependent on food and food is only grown in certain seasons. And being observers—and having the large brains that are one of the hallmarks—if you'll excuse the pun—of our species, they would certainly remember from year to year that the rains came at a certain time and the migrating animals came at a certain time and that the days grew longer at this point and the nights grew longer at another. They didn't have to look at a smartphone to know the day or the weather or where they were supposed to be. They looked to the natural world—to the skies, to the trees, to the animals.

When humans began raising permanent structures—monuments to Ancestors or deities or darned good corn crops—they raised up stone circles and burial mounds that aligned with the solstices and equinoxes—and created celestial observatories.

In the Boyne River Valley in County Meath in Ireland, there is a place called Brú na Bóinne, which contains several monuments, notably Newgrange.

Newgrange is a huge circular stone structure estimated to be 5,000 years old, older than Stonehenge, older than the Egyptian pyramids. It was built to receive a shaft of sunlight deep into its central chamber at dawn on winter solstice.

The light illuminates a stone basin below intricate carvings—spirals, eye shapes, solar disks. Maeshowe, on the Orkney Islands off Scotland, shares a similar trait, where the setting sun of the winter solstice shines down the passageway into the center of the mound.

Why? Why spend years erecting a monument—in the case of Newgrange, a monument with a corbelled stone roof that hasn't leaked in all its long history—to mark this event? Often there are burials within the massive structures, now just sad bits of bone with flashy grave goods in expensive exhibits at the visitors' center. Did the entry of the light down those narrow passageways herald a return to life for the original occupants? Did the entry of the sun represent rebirth or fertility? Was the shaft of sunlight a bridge for the dead? Did they go from home on such a bridge of light, or did they return to watch over their Descendants and their flocks and fields?

Hundreds of other megalithic structures throughout the world are oriented to the solstices and the equinoxes. And some scholars have suggested that Christian churches in medieval Europe were also solar and sometimes lunar observatories (I recommend The Sun in the Church by J.L. Heilbron). The return of light—the rebirth of the sun—the Sol Invictus of Mithras—the unconquered sun, supporter of life on the planet, without which nothing can grow, without which our tribe, in whatever way we define it, cannot continue. There's even a modern ailment that speaks to the condition: SAD (Seasonal Affective Disorder), sometimes called winter depression or winter blues. All animals react to the changing seasons with changes in mood, metabolism, and behavior, and human beings are just the same. Most people find they eat and sleep slightly more in winter and dislike the dark mornings and short days.

We can gather as a community when the moon and the sun are dark and perceive that we are in the cauldron, the crucible in which creation and destruction and re-creation are all possible and, in fact, inevitable. The cauldron is an appropriate metaphor for our work during and following the fall of our "towers."

We are not taught as children to embrace the darkness, we are not taught to think of the dark as a time of rest and peace and creative gestation. We don't consider the value of "endarkenment." Light equals good, dark equals bad, and the implications of that dualism haunt us in our political, cultural, and religious lives. The New Age movement is rightly teased for being populated by light chasers, as though there is no virtue in the darkness. But what mysteries could we explore, where could our souls journey, if we came to embrace the darkness as a natural time of renewal? If we used what nature has given us to nourish our bodies and prepare our own fields to lie fallow for a time? What wellsprings of creativity and magic might bubble up if only we could be quiet a while. Imagine leaving the hectic energies of the "holiday season" behind and coming together in community, to sit as we are sitting now, in the dark and the quiet. What things could rise unbidden, without striving, if only we give them a space in which to rise?

Silence, darkness. The concept that the dark is no less holy than the light. When we give ourselves that gift, what happens? Well, you might fall asleep. And that's no bad thing either in our hurry-up, multitasking world. To give your body and your mind and your soul a little down time, a little ahhh time. Stilling your frantic mind for a bit, taking a deep breath (take one now). Remembering what's important and what's a distraction. House still isn't clean enough for company? Haven't bought all the gifts you require yourself to give? Forgot to pay the credit card bill this month? Wonder if your beloved will make it through this season or be with you next year at this time?

Often in nature when there is silence there is watchfulness and fear. As nature beings, as Earth folk, we are as subject to this as we are to the falling of the leaves and the coming of the spring blossoms and the return of the sun. Here in this darkness, what looms in front of you? Gruesome as Fuseli's painting, what dark terror sits on your shoulder, not letting you relax or regroup or be the authentic self you want to be, that you used to be? Here in this place of silence and darkness, give up that fear to the night, let the cauldron of beginnings and endings, of death and rebirth, hold that fear for you. Allow yourself to let that fear go and let the empty space left by it—a hole with jagged edges and deep tracks—let that space fill with the possibility of something new and bright and different. Rather than bearing the ills you have, as the Bard tells us through his Danish prince, let your imagination fly to places you know not of. Name your fear and let it go.

⟨ଓଽ⟩

But now I want to talk about power and the uses of power, so I'll speak in terms of ancient struggles for autonomy and of patriarchal systems that are still to be struggled against, transformed, or overcome.

If you have not yet read Eisler's The Chalice and The Blade, pick up a used copy and begin it in the next weeks. The research in this area has gone further, but to my mind her scholarship is as strong as it ever was. Much of Wicca and Goddess worship/study in the seventies has been discredited or reimagined. If you are familiar with Merlin Stone's When God Was A Woman, you'll know that some of that work has also been discredited.

But Eisler is solid, and her reframing of "patriarchy" into notions of "power over" and hierarchy gave us a way to talk about these concepts in mixed-gendered groups. After all, it isn't about "male bashing"—though they have been the primary beneficiary of this ancient system—it's about a system that was codified into law in Sumer, made holy writ in the Pentateuch and stays with us today, part biological determination and part cultural imperative.

How do you define power? Authority? When you think of yourself, is power a part of that equation? And yes, please consider physical power as well as professional authority in your field and personal spiritual power.

Authentic Power

I had two very interesting conversations today with two old friends. Both conversations centered on the uses of power and the flow of power and authority from the core group of individuals that runs any organization. How do we—working in a consensus system—keep the flow of that energy to the people who are not the core group? How does it flow out and then back?

Two of us talked in terms of a spiral that winds in and then back out again.

I'm working with the image of the sea, the tide moving in and out, the energy moving in a continuous flow. How do you begin to structure a governing body that flows like that? When we've lived with top-down systems our whole lives, how do we create a new way of modeling power so that it empowers all the people involved in an organization?

It's a lot to think about. As we created Mother Grove Goddess Temple, literally from the ground up, we reimagined how a church can work. We didn't have many positive images and histories to work from, and it was interesting, terrifying work.

As many people suspect, Witches not only wield power, we talk about it. And as we talk about wielding it, we lament not having enough or having too much. It's a curse, really. We're just like underdressed D&D characters. You know that Texas phrase "all hat and no cattle"? Well, the Pagan community can be guilty of "all sword and no sorcery."

So we talk a lot about ethics and standards. You had no idea, did you? So many spells, so little time.

We feminists spent years sitting in empowerment circles, learning the ways of patriarchal "power over." We drew power into ourselves, discussed how women use power differently, and wondered if we would ever have the chance.

Years later, we again gathered in circles, and we imagined ourselves finally "standing in our power," whatever we thought that meant. We have come now to understand that holding power (through elected office or our personal authority and agency) isn't enough if we don't have the skill or courage to wield it.

Patriarchy has bestowed on us the simple and effective hierarchy, the symbolic hill structure of power where authority resides in the head at the top of the hill and wanders down the hill to the base, where most of us reside. That teetering king of the hill sets the agenda, and the rest of us on the slopes and terraces are expected to follow it.

We repeat this pattern too often to make light of it. It is terribly efficient. We have only to replace the head and the system goes on in its old familiar way. When the hill itself no longer seems to work, we rarely think to replace the earth works themselves. Our assumption is that a different king will make the whole thing vital again.

As these Tower Times are showing us, it is time to replace the structure of the hill. To replace it with circles of power, circles of authority that are linked into a strong chain wherein we all are a link.

We have some tools for this and through conversation and exploration can discover many more. This will require us to ground ourselves, to bring our strongest skills to focus our energy and intention.

Focus is one of the great tools in our work-basket. Like corvids, we all love the shiny, but let's work a little harder not to let it rule us. It is shiny for a reason, and that reason is rarely good. We mustn't give in to the culture's drive to control where we aim our focus.

Take time for your daily spiritual practice, whatever that may be. Sit at your home altar, walk through the woods, go to your church or temple. Pray, if you do that. Circle dance. Drum. Sing. Connect with the Divines and rest in the glorious agricultural cycle that Pagan religions are built on. That all religions are built on.

Sit upon the land where you live. Notice everything you can about it—drought or flood or perfect weather, what the birds are singing in the morning, how the air smells at the end of the day. Be outside even if the weather is uncomfortable. Pace yourself in heat and sun, splash in rain, touch leaves, walk in bare feet. Become a helpful part of your ecosystem as often as you can.

Remember that your Ancestors had a difficult time of it and still managed to produce you and your ilk. They didn't have the blessing/trauma of social media and somehow managed to know how friends and family were faring and even what their political opinions were. Amazing. They lived through the Depression and pogrom, through hunger and insecurity, through loss and slavery and exile. Buck up, in other words. Even in these times of roiling change, there is joy and music and love to be found, to be tended, to be enjoyed. Talk to your Ancestors. Ask them about fiddle music and evenings on the porch and fresh peach pie. Do that—talk to them—even if they haven't been around for centuries or you never knew them. Do that even if they are dust. Gain some perspective.

Instead of giving in to despair and fear, maybe you could do the thing you claim you do. Maybe you could do some community organizing or organic gardening or ceremony or magic. Yes, magic. You can start by setting an intention, which will require you to strategize and decide what the best course of action might be. Yes, that again. And while you're thinking of that, you could set an altar for the country you claim to have concerns about. There are plenty of examples of that in the Googleverse, but you could use your imagination—give it some exercise—and come up with a national altar. You know the colors. You know the emblems. If the national political conventions have taught us anything, it is what the symbols can be. Call in the Ancestors of the nation, however you see them. Call in the Divines that hold sway. Libertas and Columbia and Uncle Sam? Sure, why not?

And instead of wringing your hands, biting your nails, and fearing the future, engage all your resources and do some work. Yes, you. And me. And all we.

Did you forget who you are in the drama of this moment? Remember now. There is much work to do.

CHAPTER TEN

THE WEIGHT OF LETTING GO AND LETTING BE: TOO INTIMATE FOR THE AIR

I live my life in widening circles
that reach out across the world.
I may not complete this last one
but I give myself to it.
I circle around the divine,
around the primordial tower.
I've been circling for thousands of years
and I still don't know: am I a falcon,
a storm, or a great song?
—Ranier Maria Rilke

My friend is dealing with a debilitating autoimmune disease. She has met with doctors and herbalists, all in an effort to find the healing that seems so close she can almost taste it. She wakes up most mornings in intense pain, and she worries, living alone, that she is losing her sight—that she will go blind. She is a writer and a mystic. She has other ways of seeing, but the world in which we live makes those less important than the ability to get in the car and drive into town for food and companionship. She is not a woman of means and can't afford many of the treatments that are offered. And many of the treatments—like chemo—are too toxic to even contemplate.

Lately she has talked about letting go, of coming to terms with the inevitability of her condition. I can't tell if she's given up or is merely tired of the struggle for now.

What I find so inspiring about how she walks through the world is her wicked sense of humor. Those of us who know her see the struggles and the pain, feel the grief with her. And we always shriek with surprise when her hideous sense of humor erupts. She certainly does it for us, to give us some hope that all is not lost. But she says she also does it for herself. Even though she deals moment by moment with the sort of agony I wouldn't wish on my worst enemy, she finds that her funny bone can still get tickled and she can tickle it herself. I hope she never loses that, for all our sakes.

She inspires me with all that she holds on any given day, but she also inspires me with what she can let go, if only for a little while. I try to practice that and encourage you to try it too. If I had such a thing as a mantra, it would be something like taking my work seriously but myself not so much.

There is a Unitarian Universalist congregation that invites me to take the pulpit a couple of times a year and generally treats me like a member of the family. All the chalice lighting pieces and some of the essays in this book were written for that beloved congregation.

I delight in surprising them and asking them to go with me to silly or unexpected places. One year I asked them to rearrange the entire seating into a sort of semicircle, and my talk was about waking up to their role in the world. I set my phone to have a rooster's crow as its ringtone, and a member of the congregation volunteered to call me at the exact right moment. The congregation looked shocked that I had forgotten to turn off my phone, after admonishing them to do the same. But they laughed when I looked out at them while holding the ringing phone and declared, This is your wake-up call.

They have inspired me with their good and generous hearts, and I have sometimes rewarded them by scaring the pants off them. In a talk a few years ago, I ripped apart their notion of wolves as harmless and important members of the ecosystem and invited them to travel back with me to the Europe of our Ancestors where wolves were a threat, snow a deadly and regular occurrence, and losing your coal of fire a potential death sentence. This was all in an effort to remind them to be intentional about tending to each other and acknowledging their interdependence.

But I finished with a solemn warning from a television show I've never seen.

Winter has come.

I looked out at their blank, concerned faces, closed my notebook, and nodded to the pianist.

It was great.

They keenly feel the responsibility of their privilege, however, and sometimes need to be reminded of the wasted effort of guilt. And to lighten that burden of too much knowledge and not enough agency, I also like to make them smile when I can.

I played an elaborate joke on them one Samhain. They were expecting me to nag them about their Ancestors and practice my dreadful Gaeilge on them. Instead, I came in solemnly with a cardboard box, a chalice, and a framed picture, covered in cloth.

I am adding it here for you, to remind you that it is also permissible to smile and laugh during this time of falling towers. In fact, laughing and dancing and generally living a rich, full life may be the best way to counter a culture of death and destruction. This talk appealed to the congregation's highly educated minds as well as their subtle humor. The triumph of a light touch and the power of humor over guilt. I suspect you will guess the era of this ritual from the Dan Brown book and film that inspired it.

Opus Adorei

> To the Congregants:
> I have fasted, I have drunk the kykeon,
> I have completed my tasks.
> —Clement of Alexandria, Second-Century Initiate

Most of you know that I am a Witch and a Wiccan and a Priestess. I am a member of several alumnae associations, the Sierra Club, the ACLU, and a Goth club called Jolie Rouge in downtown Asheville. I am a registered Independent who leans toward the Green Party. But you may not know that I am also a member of a secret order called Opus Adorei, an order that traces its lineage back to the golden days of the Mycenaeans. When the pyramids were built, our Order was there. When the mystery religion at Eleusis—a cult so secret that we have no real information about them after all these centuries—our Order was there. Selu the Corn Mother was the icon of our Order before the Europeans arrived in North America. Opus means work. Adorei means corn.

Thanks to Dan Brown, everyone's heard of Opus Dei. Well, we predate those teenagers at Opus Dei by two millennia. So if they start their smart talk about what an old and venerated group they are, give them the raspberry. Tell them you know about Opus Adorei and they should go build a codex or something.

We have decided as an Order to reveal some of our secrets because, well, because they are just too good to keep secret anymore. Have you wondered how it is that Halloween and Samhain, the New Year and Ancestor worship, fasting and free candy—how that all works? I am here today to tell you all about it.

(I took the cover off the frame to reveal the Mona Lisa.) Look familiar? One of the prominent members of our Order was responsible for this painting. Think I'm about to talk about Leonardo? No way. He was a nice boy, a quiet teenager and so creative with his mystifying symbolism and quirky codes. But the real brain in that family was his mama, the leader of our Order from 1460 to 1500. Until very recently she was said to be a peasant girl, a barmaid, who caught the eye of Ser Piero di Antonio of Vinci. But the truth has come out at last. Caterina was an Arab slave woman from Palestine, a woman who brought together the work of Opus Adorei in Jerusalem and meshed it with the long history of the Order in Greece and Italy. With this coming together of the two strongest strains of the Order, we were poised on the brink of greatness, a new world order built upon the sharing of sweetness.

All this is encoded in the painting, a painting Leonardo did of Caterina as he remembered her from his childhood. Let's look at the message encoded in this remarkable work. Note her overall shape—made more conical by the addition of extra fabric near the waistline of her garment. The fingers of her right hand form the sacred shape. The trim on her tunic is a chain of small kernels, and that smile, that mysterious smile about which so much speculation has been... speculated? She has a mouthful of candy corn, of course.

(I revealed the candy corn.) Behold the sacred grain. You'll note its shape is rampant in the art and mathematics of the ancient world and the world of the Renaissance and Enlightenment. It is seen in the pyramids in Egypt, the megalithic tombs of Crete. We see it in the design of the perfectly planned city of Washington, DC. The Freemasons helped us with that, by the way, and it cost the Order tons of candy corn. The Washington Monument?

Why do you think he had wooden teeth? You would, too, if you ate candy corn morning, noon, and night. The shape is seen in the Great Seal, the necropolis in the Forbidden City, in Kurgan burials on the steppes of Mother Russia. In short, Opus Adorei is everywhere, and we are claiming the twenty-first century as the beginning of the Corn Millennium. Blessed be the corn!

What does all this have to do with Ancestors and the New Year? With birth and death and rebirth? The great mysteries at Eleusis reveal the story of Demeter, the Earth Goddess whose daughter Persephone descends into the underworld and is reborn. The mysteries of these rites are the evolving of life, death, and rebirth. The Earth Mother retired to Eleusis and in Her sorrow withheld the blessing of growth from all the seeds of the Earth. The rites of Eleusis were the most influential of the mystery religions. Those ceremonies were accessible to both genders, and initiates came away with a sense of security in the afterlife and a sense of the bounty guaranteed in this world. The reenactment of those mysteries symbolizes the events that constantly happen on Earth for which there is no improvement or even a need for any, for this world continues forever. The initiates, and those believing likewise, who have learned the ways of these rites come to see and know the world as it is, not through a mythological filter of guilt and sin and retribution.

This morning I invite you each to join me in a celebration of the new year and our collective Ancestors and the sweetness of life on this planet we call home. In short, I am initiating each of you into the ancient mysteries of Opus Adorei. As you each take from the wooden bowl that which is freely given, remember this, new initiates of the great mystery: there is no law greater than loving your planet. There is no rule more binding than offering and receiving hospitality. Pleasure is not a sin, feeling gratitude to your neighbors and family and Mother Earth is okay. Slowing down and appreciating the changing of the seasons is a gift to yourself and your community. Use this time, this final harvest, as the ancients used it—look back over your year and ask yourself if there are things to be undone, people unthanked to whom you owe gratitude. Did you have a crazy year full of frustrations and scary encounters? Did your life change in wonderful ways? Were things lost forever? Do you bring unnecessary baggage and heaviness with you into this new year? Spend the next few days reviewing the year and bringing yourself into right relation with your family, your community, your planet.

There is sweetness in the world—that is the lesson of Opus Adorei. The Earth is a complex ball of sweetness of which you and you and you are all a part. When we remember that—the gift of candy corn—it makes it easier somehow to forgive the jerk who cuts you off on the expressway, to accept the differences of the people you meet who are not like you. When we look at the colors of the corn—the yellow that symbolizes the golden honey sun, the orange band that symbolizes the Earth, and the white tip full of potential and possibility—we are reminded of our long history as well as the years that are to come. The cycle of the seasons continues year after year, and the bounty of the Earth supports and nurtures us.

What is there to fear when we are part of such a web of life? What can we not do when we work together as a community to bring honor to our Ancestors, healing to our environment, and peace to our species? It doesn't take a cryptic code or a codex or a secret society. Take the gift of the corn; give the gift of the corn. No mystery, really. Be kind, love deeply, laugh when you can. Don't sweat the small stuff and know that when the heavy big stuff hits, you are not alone.

Happy New Year, initiates. May it be ever sweet.

CHAPTER ELEVEN

LIGHTING THE SIGNAL FIRES AND GROWING CIRCLES ON THE GROUND

*Think of the wonderful circles in which our whole being moves
and from which we cannot escape no matter how we try.
The circler circles in these circles.*
—E. T. A. Hoffmann

Circles on the ground. We have come to the end of this portion of the book. This is the place where we look for some support and ideas—and something like hope.

When social media contacts ask me about the process of this thing I call Tower Time, I point them to the document file that you will find as an addendum to this book. I've added files as inspiration hits me or an experience dictates.

When colleagues and friends ask the same thing, we go deeper. We meet for coffee or Guinness, and we get down to specifics.

Resilience in the face of change is the answer to so many things in life. It is a truism that most people fear and "hate" change, but change is also the very essence of natural systems. Without change, often massive change, the biosphere cannot prosper nor continue. Much of our loathing of change comes in our uncertainty about our ability to endure it: the whitewater that requires us to look only forward, the dragon ride that requires us to close our eyes and cling to the scaly back of change.

121

This is a perfectly apt response because sometimes we or they or it don't survive change, not in any recognizable form. When we embrace the cyclical nature of everything we know, however, we come to a place where we can stand in the face of the change and move through it to the next place.

Mostly the changes that roll over us or that we move through don't destroy us. They change us. For better or worse and sometimes in unimaginable ways, they change us. They encourage us to strategize about effective means of doing what we're set on doing.

In Henrik Ibsen's play *Peer Gynt*, our hapless wanderer confronts the Bøyg, a character from Scandinavian folklore whose role is to throw up obstacles along a traveler's path. Peer struggles with his inability to remove this burden from his homeward path until he realizes that the answer is not to fight his way through but to go around.

Our work here requires many things from us, but the most important may be the ability to think of other ways of doing the thing that we feel is the right thing to do in a given situation. This mental and emotional flexibility—twinned with our own ethical sense and boundaries (and a sense of humor)—will go far in making this new world, in creating these circles on the ground.

For us, the Bøyg can be the emotional controls that were set into us long ago, through family, experience, and culture. As we ponder whether we must go around or over or through our own Bøyg, let's look at some of those engineered traits that can stop us in our tracks.

Guilt, or how do you get rid of carrying the guilt of everything?

First you have to realize that guilt is an emotion that feels like an action. When you realize that—and when you know you have some sort of agency in a situation—

then you can choose to do something about it instead of feeling something. Agency is the ability to change what must be changed. Sometimes we don't have that as individuals and must reach out to colleagues and friends to buttress us and give our work the rocket fuel it needs.

Shame is rage suppressed through inaction. It is a burden that is heavy as concrete, that constricts around the heart and drives us to a painful ennui. Shame is often used to control the actions of others by reminding them of their inadequacies, publicly and privately. It is a technique, like gaslighting, that allows those who inflict it to step back from responsibility for their actions.

Regret is intense and directed sadness that comes from a failure of discernment and clear action. Not as crippling as shame or grief, regret affords us a lingering look into the possibilities of a lost past, one in which we failed to do "the right thing."

Despair comes from finally giving in and giving up but feeling the grief of that. Despair is grief left unvoiced.

Fury. Who among us has not felt the delicious flush of righteous anger, of fury set free of its cultural moorings? The Greeks understood "furies" to be avenging spirits, the Erinyes who regularly appear in classical plays as a kind of deus ex machina to run the plot onto a sandbar.

Forgetting and remembering. We crave the familiar, we humans. Even when the familiar is unpleasant, even painful. We long for the fantasy childhoods of fiction and gentle story, often forgetting the still-covered darkness that we have covered and tried to forget. All of us carry old wounds, long-buried and unexamined traumas. We are triggered in our interactions with our kindred, and we overreact, protecting that distant child in her shocking vulnerability.

Many of us continue to excavate those old earth works of our earlier lives, engaging in the seemingly never-ending work of making ourselves whole by some measurable level.

CRSO

Over the years, I have surprised so many of my coreligionists by acknowledging that I am a reincarnation agnostic. I simply don't "believe" in reincarnation, especially as presented in soft and easily digestible New Age publications. But the real reason I am not a believer is both more understated and more mystical.

I was fortunate to have a brilliant woman named Jyoti Bryan as my physics tutor for well over a year, before she faced her final illness. We explored the universe over coffee and traveled concepts of both time and space while also eating sandwiches. There were books, of course—I still have them around here somewhere, dog-eared, annotated, and bristling with colored flags.

But the books were secondary to the conversation, to the words of a woman whose thoughts were deep and broad, a woman who invited me to think in dimensions I never imagined. As a theatre artist, I had always struggled with linearity, and physics set my mind free from all the notions of time I had ever known.

I am not a believer in reincarnation because we don't know how time works or its effects on living systems or indeed mythic ones.

I've written all this by way of inviting you to reconsider what you know of time as it applies to the remaking of our culture. Is it too late? Is time up?

You say you want a revolution.

Well, maybe not.

We all want to change the world, but...

Social media platforms these days contain more than adorable kitty antics and photos of people's meals. The subtle distress call that flared with the Occupy movement and continued with Black Lives Matter, #MeToo, and the Dakota pipeline has become a signal fire, flashing across the hilltops. Spend any time at all on Facebook, Twitter, Instagram, and the rest, and you will be informed (and often berated) by self-proclaimed social justice warriors who want nothing more than to drive their readers to a fever pitch of anxiety and heartbreak. Those touchscreen revolutionaries rarely have solutions to problems but do know how to drive their readership to a place of frustration and guilt. What can we do when we have little or no agency in a given situation? How do we function in a society where our purity on any given issue is constantly challenged? Where our half-hearted, awkward attempts at cultural change are met with cold disdain?

Each time a new calendar year begins, we breathe in the freshness—the cold, icy freshness—of renewed possibility and culturally approved change. We are encouraged to make impossible vows about our health or finances or relationships. In these hectic times, many of us don't resolve to do much more than hold on to the shards of the world we knew, the sharp-edged pieces of our cracked lives—and try to keep from falling from the edges of the flat and tilting world.

What if we turned this idea of resolution—or being stern in our resolve and implacable in our quest for personal betterment—what if we turn the old idea of New Year's resolutions on its ear and pondered the possibilities involved in this new revolution of the planet around the sun?

Revolution isn't simply a rebellion against oppression, as you know. And for those of you who are puzzlers and scrabblers and such—who love the play of language and the flexibility and general weirdness of English—what else does the word "revolution" suggest to you? Set this book down and stand up. Turn in place. Notice how the vista constantly changes as you widen your gaze, revolving. What do you notice as you slowly turn? Now revolve again and see how the details begin to show themselves.

When my Goddess-daughter Geneva was little, she loved spinning in a chair backstage at what is now the Hazel Robinson amphitheater. She was generally spun once, gently. But she was insistent, as children often are— more! more!—and she got a good long spin, which was not good for her tummy. You have not lived, friends, until you have scraped sad vomit from your Elizabethan costume after you have comforted a very green four-year-old.

In spite of this sticky trip down my personal memory lane, I invite you to throw caution to the wind as we face down the fear and perceived lack of agency in these Tower Times. These times within this culture may require us to spin very fast indeed, and finding our way through those passages is part of the intent of this book.

You can climb to a hill or go to a downtown rooftop in an elevator and look straight out in front of you for the view. Then turn to your right. And again. And again. And finally around to the original spot. New views, new vistas. Something different at each place. A chance to inhabit a different locale and to look with fresh eyes.

What can these new vistas reveal about ourselves, our cultures, and our journey? And what skills do we need to have to navigate these new worlds with grace and clarity, to bring back to our own hearths the visions and the answers?

Here are some possibilities.

Beginner Mind

I learned this as a Buddhist concept—the idea of
starting fresh with a beginner mind. It feels light and easy
to me, but golly, it never is. I have too many dearly loved
bits of culture or traditions or personal history that seem
to cling to my mind like barnacles. It is really difficult
to see a situation or a place or a person with new eyes.
And sometimes we're simply stubborn and don't want
to do it. I write about the rural/urban divide—and have
done more so since the last national election. We like to
compartmentalize things, and frankly, social interaction
is usually easier if we can pigeonhole a new situation
or new person and think no more deeply about it. We
can file that person away as a flake, an earth mother,
homeless, a hippy, an anarchist, a healer, a freak. Then
we go on to use our brainpower for something more
important.

More important. Think about that for a moment.
What can be more important in social interactions than
giving the others involved the gift of your deep attention
and the grace of your compassionate understanding?

New situations—job or church or being pulled over
for speeding—often bring sharp pangs of insecurity, even
anxiety. There are people who suffer from agoraphobia,
but for most of us, we are called to bring our hearts into a
given situation and use our good brains to think through
before giving in to fear that can lead to unreasoning
anger.

Setting Boundaries

This is my personal and ongoing work, and I confess
I am really, really not good at it. As the adult daughter of
alcoholics, I was trained from an early age to please all

those around me, to placate, to be selfless. And until very recently, I tended to an elderly friend whose demands for care were sharp and insistent—so much so that I always left the ring function activated on my phone overnight in case her blood sugar bottomed out and I had to make a run for it.

I have some difficulty in saying no to things I don't want to do and often remain in unstable and unhealthy relationships in an effort to heal them.

That's me—does it sound like you? If it does, then I invite you to join me as I learn the fine art of No Saying and Boundary Setting. I'm starting with some talking points for those times when I'm asked to do or be or opine on something quickly.

- That is fascinating. Let me give that some thought.
- I will take this to my home altar and approach it prayerfully.
- Really interesting. Let me cogitate on it.

Buying time, friends, just buying a little time, like we used to count to ten before losing our tempers.

Some of you will not need that. Setting boundaries is a strategy that has either come easy to you or that you have learned in the fiery classrooms of personal experience. But if you do, buy yourself some time as you set some boundaries. Are you the go-to person in any activity? Do people say you're a natural leader? Are you "reliable?"

Are you your own backup when you ask someone else to do anything?

Practice with me now, those who need to.

- No.
- No, thank you.

• I have too much on my plate right now, but thank you for thinking of me.

Be flattered, respond with kindness but firmness. Let others learn to harness their own reliability. Take back some parts of your life and use them for living and loving and dancing and laughing and eating yummy things. Knock some stuff off your calendar. Give yourself the gift of your own life and your own unfrazzled company.

Laying Down Burdens

"These mountains that you are carrying, you were only supposed to climb."

—Najwa Zebian

When I sit with people who are seeking a listening ear or some gentle advice, they often tell of traumas from years past that continue to color, to haunt their lives. That is the unraveling work that all humans do as a result of living in families, in communities, in a culture broken in so many ways.

But I also hear about burdens carried long past their sell-by date. I think of Jacob Marley from *A Christmas Carol* with his chains and metal boxes.

"You are fettered," said Scrooge, trembling. "Tell me why?"

"I wear the chain I forged in life," replied the ghost. "I made it link by link, and yard by yard; I girded it on of my own free will, and of my own free will I wore it."

What are we all carrying in our stone-filled suitcases that we can reasonably set down, possibly forever? Slights and insults from broken people, unfair treatment that can't be remedied or maybe it was?

At the beginning of classes and retreats I lead, I will often assure people that they can leave the burdens of the week at the door for the duration of our time together, to free them to be truly present for the work in which we'll engage. And when our time together is over, I like to remind them of how light they felt without that bag of regrets and old grief... and that they can leave it at the door for the Earth to compost. Sometimes that even works.

Set them down, those old woundings. Leave them there and pick up your hard-earned wisdom on the way out.

Tend Your Body, Tend Your Community, Tend Your Land

The word tender, like "revolution," has several meanings. It implies softness and the ability to be malleable. Money is legal tender. And a person who takes loving care of something or someone else is also a tender. When I write and teach about Tower Time, there is often a place in that conversation for self-care. Resting when you can't sleep, eating nutritious foods, strengthening your body and mind through gentle exercise, drinking water. That is self-tending, and we as a community need you to tend to yourself. And good self-tending almost always leads to a robust notion of community tending: making the world more equitable for all its beings, making our town, our county, our state, and our country a place where justice prevails. Sharing all that zucchini in the dog days of August—that, too, is community tending. Sitting at the kitchen table with a friend and a cuppa tea and listening, really listening, ditto.

When it comes to tending the land, that comes in many forms too. From recycling to off-grid living, from community gardens to wilderness retreats, we plug ourselves back into our place in the biosphere. In tribal times, all of Earth was spirited, peopled with spirits indigenous to a particular place.

There are still some places in the world where the country folk will talk about how a certain area is peopled by ghosts or little people, but the larger culture has mostly lost the notion of a place having a soul. Let us now be part of the re-sacralizing of the landscape as we tend the land.

Hold Fast All That is Good

I have a funny little ginger jar that has this motto emblazoned across its blue shoulders. And it always reminds me to look for the good in people, in places, in things. That holding on—holding fast—to the best of us is the only way I know to keep that little fire burning. It is so easy to get discouraged, to grow weary, to give up. And sometimes we do have to give up on an idea or a person because it no longer enriches our lives. In friendship and kinship, we have come to know that there are people we love but with whom we cannot be in a relationship. And we let that clinging go so that only the love remains.

What is good in your world? What feels wholesome and nourishing? Who and what nurtures you? Honor those things and beings. Hold them close. Ponder them in your heart.

It's a beginning, in this time of falling towers. In reading these words, you hopefully have already come up with a hundred more ways to revolve your thinking and revolve your life.

Good for you. Carry on.

As I write this, it is January, as cold a one as most of us natives can remember. It is the beginning of the calendar year—a time for renewal as well as regret. It is where we stand at this moment—on the knife-edge of history and prophecy, like Roman Janus peering both forward and back.

May the fierce winds that break the trees and freeze the rivers blow fear and anxiety away from your hearth and your heart. May you feel the strength of your soul, your back, and your purpose. May song and laughter fill the air around you, like the champagne bubbles of old New Year's eve, and may your feet never be too achy to dance a step.

You say you want a revolution? Then bring one. These are the times we were made for.

Others are writing about and will write about these changing times. Some of them will use the same language you find throughout these pages, and some will explore different ways of expressing the same thought. Already there was the panel at the American Academy of Religion conference, and there are monographs and articles showing up in my social media feeds, and more are no doubt on the horizon. Others will explain the whys and the wherefores in more academic terms. Some will argue finer points as well as the overall concept of Tower Time itself. This is an idea with legs, a thought that deserves more thinking, more writing.

This book is from me to you. I have written it in my own style and in my own way, and it has taken me years to get it to this place—where you are holding it in your hands or reading it on your electronic device.

You will also write the next chapters, the new books, as you make this liminal place your home base. You will call together circles, that scheme and plan and do—and you will stand under a dark night sky to remember all the Ancestors that came before you.

And all of us will live the next chapters as we weave together allies and neighbors, learn old skills, reach across socioeconomic boundaries to forge a new world in iron and ice and fire.

Because this is different, this one. It has been building like an ancient relentless tsunami for so many generations, so many moon cycles. The energy surges not from the top down, not from the capitol to the wildlands, not from the civic plaza to the hearth. Reverse it. From heart to hearth to town square to county seat to state capitol to the boggy seat of the republic.

We have brought a battering ram shaped like Eve and Gaia and Grandma to the gates of power. Wherever those gates stand. Even if they stand in our own souls.

It doesn't begin today, with this book. It continues, this work of many hands and hearts. Spiral in, spiral out. A clockwork of deepest freedom, of desire, of joy. We are come to kick it down. And to dance on the ashes. And to rebuild the world. Breathe deep. Ground yourself in the dear old Earth.

Today, with one foot in the beginning and one foot in the end, straddling the doorway... today reach out with your hands and seize this time. Balance your expectations and your fears, your courage and your vulnerability.

Holding fast to all those possibilities, feel the dear Earth's energy flow up and through you, strengthening you, remembering you.

You got this, this transiting white water. It's Tower Time, as you well know.

Looking forward and holding fast to the good, the real.

The energy is ratcheting up. Edges are crumbling. The center can't hold.

Or can it? You know what to do, beloveds. Pull up a swift protective circle and arrange your magics according to your skills. Gather what you need from the hedges and edges. Create your clockwork shambles and set them in motion.

Join me now, in the center, in the heart, of this great working. We stand shoulder to shoulder with our kindred, our Ancestors, the ageless spirits of the land. We are a mighty cohort, patient, waiting.

A chord is struck. A bodhran speaks. The little pipes begin, and the great pipes warm up. We are readying ourselves for the exquisite moment.

Hold fast. Fear not. It is time.

ᚳᚱᚹᚩ

Night has fallen in the southern highlands of the old Appalachian Mountains.

In my house, we have replaced the furnace, long to ready the gardens, and are preparing for our annual celebration of Rev. Charles Bryan at Burns Night.

This day has brought what we need and, for some of us, what we want. There is the usual wild swing among emotions on social media and in society. There is mourning and fury and joy and satisfaction.

Today I heard a train whistle and a love song and a woodpecker in the maple tree.

And I heard you.

We are standing at the gates, the great pipes skirling around us. We are fearless and proud, farseeing, strategic, cunning. There is a culture to heal and a world to build. There is healing to be found in the darkness, nestled in mystery. You are the weaver and the healer, the web and the seeker.

This is not easy. It is heartbreaking as well as backbreaking. We will lose people and places and traditions. We may lose ourselves, and we will find ourselves. With any luck, we may weave together resilient and egalitarian communities—the "tribes" we so often reference—as joyous places for our Descendants to dwell and a source of pride for our Ancestors to ponder.

Change. Transition. Opportunity. Yes and yes. We are charged to tend the biosphere, which includes the land and the water and the beings and all. Not to be superior to it but to acknowledge that we are a part of it—a damaging and dangerous part. We will gulp our mea culpas and put on our work gloves and change the world.

We can do this. You can do this. It isn't about a big central authority or a savior or a miracle. It is about circles on the ground and hard work. It is about joy and life and holding fast.

Tower Time. Engage it. Own it. These are the times we were made for.

Hold fast. Breathe deep. Fear not.

Good luck.

BERMS: CREATING CEREMONIES FOR AND WITH YOUR COMMUNITY

What is a berm? I was introduced to the word "berm" a few years back. It is mostly used as a landscaping term now, but it has its origins in the great earthworks of years past as the space between a wall and a ditch. Anyone who has encountered the enormous ditch-and-bank constructions of Neolithic Europe will have some respect for the effectiveness of such a landscape feature. In researching the word—and whether it was the right one to use in this section of the book— I also discovered that in the terrible trench warfare of the War to End All Wars, it referred to the lip of the trench, the place the men leaned on to shoot at the enemy or to feel a little sunlight on their pale and weary faces.

Both things seemed good to me, so I decided to call this collection of rituals after those useful creations. Because rituals can act as a bulwark against the predations of a culture in recalibrating collapse while also serving as a place for the participants to rest for a moment while gathering the energy from their community and their Divines to go on.

This is a collection of rituals that I have written—sometimes with colleagues—and facilitated over the years I've stood as clergy for my community. I have mostly removed the names of those involved so that the ceremony seems more universal, but in a few instances, it wasn't possible.

These are real rituals that honored real events. If you have need of them and find them appealing, please feel free to adapt them to your specific needs or to be inspired by my fumblings to create your own.

I have divided them into eight sections. There are a few rituals in each section, and the last one has some odds and ends that can be used wherever you choose to use them.

You will find some repetition here. I often steal from a previous ritual for a new one and some rituals—the personal bonding ones in particular—reuse parts that I have found to work particularly well.

I encourage you to add music and movement to rituals where needed. And I often like for the participants to take something tangible home with them (candle, glass bead, length of yarn) to remind them of their experience.

- Memorials
- Samhain, Ancestors and the Dead
- Passages
- Ordination
- Seasonal
- Homely
- Dedications
- Helpful Bits and Pieces

Why is it important to celebrate together, in public? Because it is a forge that creates and strengthens community and is a crucible in which we can create something meaningful together.

Now that you've made it through this exploration of what these cultural changes imply—and have marched to the top of the ramparts of our earthworks—you may be feeling the need to stretch your muscles and make your own rituals in your own community. I've given you some examples and there are even more here, but don't let these limit you in any way. There are always reasons to come together in community. You can look to the cycles of the agricultural year as our Ancestors did. You can look to the passages within our lives. Humans do such interesting things, and you can create a rite to honor whatever those things are. I'm not suggesting you become the greeting cards business, but honestly, I can't think of anything you couldn't create a ritual around. It's about remembering, honoring, commemorating, celebrating. Creating a place where the emotional needs of the participants are met in a way that feels natural and is holistically communal. Whether a large group or an intimate setting, creating a ritual for the occasion can be as simple as lighting a beautiful candle or spending weeks preparing the robes and room décor. I suggest you do a little of both—and everything in between.

Full moon. New moon. Dark moon. The first appearance of Orion in the winter sky. The three days of meteor showers with the Leonids.

How about the first spinach of the season? The day it was warm and dry enough to work the soil in the spring is worthy of much celebration.

We are sometimes called on to facilitate the community's grief or outrage or excitement. As needed in times of disaster or community grief or celebration, we may be called on to "put something together" that will gather a community into a place of comfort and corporate intention.

Some rituals are intensely personal but best in community. Handfastings are a good example. There are many kinds of places that can be used for these berms of ours. You may have a dedicated space, but consider whether that space is sufficient. How big is the ritual? How many are likely to attend? How will you publicize it, if it is indeed a ceremony open to the public? Is there enough parking?

The types of spaces that can be used are basically two—publicly owned (city and county park and other green spaces, library meeting rooms, public schools are examples) and privately owned places (private homes or private land).

If you do not want your ritual to be interrupted, check to see whether or not a permit or insurance is required. Just check. The last thing you want is for the local constabulary to show up with a bullhorn while you are quietly honoring the dead. Your town's website may give you all the information you need, but it is also wise to find out from the police or the sheriff what is required. If you can form a relationship with them—as we did in our community—you may also choose to let them know where you'll be and what you are doing, in case you need them. Seriously. We have been protected in our First Amendment rights on more than one occasion by the intervention of the local police department. This may not be true where you are, but it is worth it to find out.

Wrangle as many volunteers as you can muster. Don't try to do these on your own. They can help with setup and takedown, with traffic and with security. You will want at least one person who is not involved in the ritual to keep eyes on the perimeter, just in case of interruption.

When the world presses in—whether it is a natural disaster or a community bereavement, you may choose to ritualize the time as a way to facilitate healing and to allow your community to stand together in shared thought and emotion.

The Dakota Pipeline Action at Standing Rock required a water ritual, which we replicated on the banks of the French Broad River. When the incompetence of corporate culture polluted the drinking water in West Virginia, we sent donations of bottled water, but we also did ritual. When two young women whom we knew were murdered, it brought a sense of agency for us to come together to honor them and to rage against what had happened to them.

BERM: MEMORIALS

Beth and her mother sometimes participated in full moon ceremonies at Mother Grove. Beth had been battling addiction for many years, and when she unexpectedly died of an overdose, the need to express our fear and sadness and anger was sharp and immediate. We sat with her family. We created with them a fitting memorial for this young woman and her too-short life. It was a celebration, but it was also a place for public grief.

I find that the trend toward "celebrations of life" that are mostly sticky-sweet PowerPoint shows without much depth leave many people feeling unfulfilled. Few people want "old-fashioned" funerals with a hired preacher who didn't know the deceased, featuring recorded versions of "Amazing Grace," and set in a generic funeral home chapel. Mourners need a place, frankly, to mourn, and sometimes that mourning is best done in a safe and public setting.

Here are some examples of funerary rites.

From the time she first sought treatment, (Name) and her family were honest with each other as much as possible about her illness. Addiction is a raw and painful and messy thing.

(Name) has always been exceptionally proud of her brother's talent as a musician, and during her time in treatment, she adopted his song as her personal anthem. She loved this song, and playing it here today is his gift to his sister. Like her illness, and under these circumstances, it is raw and painful and messy, but it is our deeply held belief that (Name) has risen up beyond the pain and sorrow that held her captive here and finally is free.

The ceremony continued with special songs, poems, and memories.

The following is a slightly different format because the family felt it was important for the gathering to begin with a big potluck. It was the perfect way to begin the public commemoration of this woman who loved to feed people. She was also a gardener, and the gathering ended with the family giving flats of young plants to the mourners.

Elegy in Shades of Green

Welcome.

Officiant: On behalf of the family, let me welcome you to this celebration—yep, celebration—of all that (Name) was to us. Well, maybe not all—because we need to be out of here by seven. As she would no doubt insist, we are going to eat first. Of course. Then we'll circle up and share some stories and some love and support for all of us who are here without our dear friend. I invite you all now to take a deep and cleansing breath and hold in your mind the image of a woman who couldn't bear people to be hungry, and let that sweet image bless the food we share today.

Mangia!

Following the potluck, we assembled to begin our commemoration.

Officiant: You have come to the end of this pathway in a journey to which we bear witness. You have come to the end of a pathway that is barred with a gate and a door. May this door open swiftly and silently. May this gate give you a moment's grace in which to rest your spirit before you venture through.

When (Name) and I talked about this gathering, she insisted that there be an "elegy," not a "eulogy." A traditional elegy is a memory poem and a doorway to remembrance, so we will begin with that today. With her elegy in shades of green.

(A poem by Mary Oliver was read.)

Too soon, too soon. How often have we all muttered that in these past few days? (Name)—our sister, our teacher, our wild child with dirty hands and grubby feet. The one who taught us unconditional love even if it was sometimes through clenched teeth.

And look at this circle of (Name)-people here. Look at us. Gardeners and poets, artists and lovers—all here because we can't quite believe it yet. Can't quite wrap our heads around it—a world without her, seeds that won't be planted, souls that won't be soothed, hugs left unhugged, smooches left unsmooched.

Dang, she was a force of nature, wasn't she? I'm watching so many of you nod. Difficult to stand up to, to disagree with because she knew what was needed and she rarely budged from that. I don't want to say stubborn exactly... but yeah...

When I think of my dear green friend, the word that always comes first is "healer," and someone posted this in social media upon learning of her death—

A true healer does not heal you; she simply reflects back to you your innate capacity to heal. She is a reflector—or a loving transparency.

A true teacher does not teach you; she does not see you as inherently separate from her or less than her. She simply reflects back your own inner knowing and reminds you of the vastness of your being. She is a mirror, a signpost.

And love is the space in which all of this is possible; love heals, and we learn best in a loving field, no threat of failure, no punishment.

So today we celebrate the juicy life of our friend, and each of us has a different piece to bring to the picture. I'll say a few more words as you gather your thoughts, and then we'll share stories as we shared food, to honor and rejoice in this life too richly lived.

One of the ways to thrive in difficult and challenging times is through listening—to your heart, to your family and tribe, to the earth and your ancestors. Real listening begins in a hard place—hearing things you don't want to hear, deep listening without frantically trying to fix things, lingering in the mystery.

We all have so much work to do, as (Name) showed us through her profound example. The brokenness of the culture we live in can only be mended, I suspect, by those of us who have been broken by it and somehow glued the bits together enough to stand upright, lock arms with our kindred, and stumble forward, dancing.

(Here I read "Wild Geese" by poet Mary Oliver.)

As we hold the family and each other in the sadness of this day, let's hear the stories of our friend in all the ways we had the privilege and pleasure to know.

Who'd like to start?

Benediction

Officiant: We are the keepers of the flame. As we stand under the summer's sunshine, we also look for lights that proclaim freedom and hope, passion and warmth. The flame is the central symbol in many of the world's faith traditions—a flame that is the light of freedom and truth—and within the halo of its glowing is the place where peace can be waged, justice served, and community built. We are the keepers of the flame, as our friend was a keeper of this green and eternal flame. We leave this holy place, beneath a waxing moon, knowing that we travel forth as kindred spirits, bound by our love and respect for this truly amazing woman. The flame we hold today in her memory and honor will bring clarity and, even if it is extinguished, we will carry it still, each to each, in brightness and trust and love. Be the light, dear friends, to hold her memory in brightness. May you always keep the flame. Blessed be.

The following poems were shared by their authors who were among those gathered. The first one is mine.

Soil Mother

There is a bear at the back door.
Blackberry jam is simmering on the stove waiting
Waiting
Waiting
For that perfect moment
not too runny, not too stiff.
The greenhouses are overflowing.
Green allies in small black pots
Wait to be rehomed in other soils
In public housing gardens
In community gardens
In new gardens
In wild gardens.
In the crowded closet there is a dark vest
From other and darker times
It is heavy as shame
Built to protect her strong and
Fierce heart
From a shot fired in strange love
And fear of women making
Choices.
Eat! Cook! Grow! Love!
Live bigger than you can reach

And give all
All
All
For love of the greenness of the world
For its sweetness
For its grace.

Beth Phipps was a daughter to the deceased and shared this piece:

When a wise woman passes...

The trees bend with the weight of forgotten fruit untouched.
The river flows backward in time to wash away empty
forgotten laundry baskets.
The flowers bloom slow to bask in the fragrance left by her
apron.
The soil itself becomes heavy with the weight of the tears left
by the living.
When a wise woman passes...
The Earth skips a rotation to rewind to the hour her laughter
rang through the blue skies.
The stars blink in rhythm to the memories sent up from the
family she honored.
When a wise woman passes...
We are left to spread their wisdom like seeds in that wet soil,
by that river, to make that tree grow
To share that fruit...
—Beth Phipps aka Sisterdiscordia

Memorial Gathering

The following ritual was partly created by the deceased herself. She had a long and gracious dying, tended by birth as well as chosen family. She remained at home, and her house in the weeks before her death from cancer was a joyful, blessed place. Hers was the most beautiful and peaceful body I have ever tended.

Set altar, water at podium, signs for family pews, smudge and call quarters at five thirty; musicians arrive at six, choir six forty-five.

Officiant: Good evening, dear friends, and welcome to a celebration of the deep and rich life of _____. Now is a good time to turn off your mobile phones—thanks. And thank you to _____ and the circles of support and love that are her family and friends. We also want to acknowledge her family and their special place in her lively life.

We are here to honor all that she was and is and to connect with the people whose lives are richer for having known her. We have chosen some short pieces to share with you—reflective of some of her many facets. We will all share songs and stories of this remarkable woman. We'll finish up by sharing food and viewing a loving video tribute to all that was and is our dear friend and sister.

Teach and sing "The River She is Flowing."

Read Poem.

Segue to how her wild and precious life affected us, personal reflections and stories, asked that they keep them brief. Stories from those gathered.

Sahara Peace Choir: "Come Spinning Down and Breaths."

Poem.

Officiant invites further comments, stories.

Second story segment fifteen to twenty minutes.

Officiant introduces the final prayer.

One of the funeral planners and I alternated lines in the funerary prayer.

You have come to the end of this pathway
In a journey to which we bear witness.

You have come to the end of a pathway
That is barred with a gate and a door.
May this door open swiftly and silently.
May this gate give you a moment's grace
In which to rest your spirit before you venture through.
We stand here with you, as your companions,
As your family, for you are beloved.
But, for now, we must remain here.
We cannot go with you to this old land.
Not yet.
For you will see the Ancestors.
You will see the Beloved Dead.
You will walk among the Divine Beings
That guide and nurture us all.
You go to dwell in the lands
Of summer and of apples
where we dance
forever youthful, forever free.
(Until your return)
We can hear the music in the mist
The drums that echo our sad hearts.
We can see your bright eyes and your smile.
And so we open the gate
We push back the door
We hold the gate open
We glance through the doorway
And with love and grief and wonder
We watch you walk through.
Hail the Traveler!
All those remembered in love, in honor,
Live on.
Farewell, o best loved,
O fairest,
Farewell.

Officiant: Thank you for sitting in this circle of love and grace tonight. We invite you now to refresh yourselves as we break bread together and then return to the sanctuary to watch the loving video tribute. Blessed be.

Ceremony for the Outcast Dead

For several years now, we have facilitated an annual memorial for those who have died alone, unloved, unwanted. It takes place in a public park near the center of our downtown. We set up a small table with candles and drip guards, small glass beads, and some candles in holders. There is a cauldron full of water, standing at the foot of the table. The number of officiants varies every year, as does the ceremony itself.

Ingathering. A simple chant encourages the attendees to let down their guard.

Welcome. Invite people to take a candle/drip guard.

There is a brief exploration of what it means to die alone or in exile. Another officiant defines "outcast" and suggests what "othering" does to individuals and communities. Officiant leads a guided meditation to walk them through the gate/doorway.

Song. "Swing Low, Sweet Chariot." Sing while lighting candles.

We each take turns singing the names of the dead we know as we drop a bead into the cauldron of water.

Finish with a prayer for the dead.

BERM: SAMHAIN, THE ANCESTORS, AND THE DEAD

Set up a big, bright colorful altar. Set out luminaria outside. Arrange an informal drum circle (if folks show up with drums).

Smudge and anoint.

Welcome.

Temple talk, in which someone from the temple's governing body expresses the need for donations.

Raise Circle.

We start in the North. Listen. (pause) Dirt and stone, tree and leaf. Standing stones on barren hilltops. Deep rotting leaves smell of the next and new season. Ancestors in the North—land of rime and ice! Ancestors of the North, hail and welcome!

Face the East now. Listen. (pause) Wind and smoke, shiver and song. Screaming gale ripping through the eaves. Bonfire smoke stinging our eyes as we look to a new year. Ancestors of the East—land of breeze and hurricane! Ancestors of the East, hail and welcome!

Face the South now, turn, turn. Listen. (pause) Flame and light, heat and scorch. Molten stone rips through the heart of mountains, flows to the sea. Scry the fire for future wisdom, distant dreams. Ancestors of the South—land of bonfire and lava! Ancestors of the South, hail and welcome!

Last is West, turn now. Turn. Listen. (pause) River and sacred well, flood and hot springs. Geyser erupts from the Earth's breast, steam and water. The path of the dead flows over the sea and into the West. Tonight we call them home. Ancestors of the West—land of the dead, island of time! Ancestors of the West, hail and welcome!

And now we turn, turn, turn to the center, and we call the Crone. Listen. We call the Hag in her wisdom and her weakness. We welcome the mothers of death and the ocher-painted faces of the warrior women. Scrawny neck and bone fingers, come home, Mother! Bride of Darkness, we carry you over the threshold. Sisters of evermore, crows on your shoulders, rise here and come home! Come home! (repeat and get the group to chant with Come home!) And so it is. You are welcome. A piece about the season of reckoning, by Patricia Monaghan, is read.

One officiant talks about Samhain, another talks about Hallowe'en, a third talks about Maman Brigitte.

Attendees are encouraged to talk about their beloved dead.

A circle dance with the dead is danced.

An officiant introduces the concept of the silent supper, and a plate of food for the dead goes on the altar; the attendees are encouraged to bless the food.

An officiant introduces the celebration of New Year. All the candles but one are extinguished. When all lights are out, we talk about the New Year and winter coming.

Finish with the following: Because our Ancestors trusted that darkness becomes light and that the wheel will always turn, here as the darkness and winter are set to engulf our world, we celebrate the new year. As the light grows from the center out, let the warmth and light within our hearts turn the wheel into a new year and bless our earth with health and vigor.

Officiants: Blessed be. Happy New Year!

Then we light one candle from the altar and light candles that have been handed to ritual-goers.

Sing "Auld Lang Syne" and wish everyone happy New Year.

Release the Circle

We start in the West. Turn there. Look—the dead are dancing, the dead are singing. They welcome our love and revel in our attention. River and sacred well, flood and hot springs. Water people, spirit people, blessed be!

To the South now, turn. Look—the dead are warming their cold hands at the bonfire, the bonefire. They welcome our warmth and hospitality. Flame and light, heat and scorch. Fire people, spirit people, blessed be!

East, to the East. Turn. Look—the breeze blows their shreds of clothing, lifts the lifeless hair. They welcome our words and songs. Wind and smoke, shiver and song. Wind people, spirit people, blessed be!

Back to the North, to the North, turn. Look—the dead are beating drums, the dead are trancing into the Earth. They are laughing at their own jokes and winking at us. Dirt and stone, tree and leaf. Bone people, spirit people, blessed be!

To the center, see the people, turning, turning, turning. She is here. See Her? Bone Woman! Old-Killt Grandma! Killer, birther, Ocher Sister. We kiss your cold cheek, we welcome your stiff embrace. Sacred Hag and Mother Crone, blessed be!

The Ancestor Vigil

We have done this Ancestor Vigil in various forms for over two decades. It is not a Samhain ritual but a vehicle for Ancestor veneration.

Altar: sugar skulls, white candles, pomegranate and apples, chalice and paten, St. Death candles.

Smudge and anoint; invite folks to put something on the altar.

Call quarters.

I invoke the powers of the North: by the Earth that nurtures us, by the bones that give us form, by the deep and ancient force that moves the universe. Guardians of the North, we welcome you.

I invoke the powers of the East: by the Air that sustains us, by the wings of our imagination, by the gentle breezes and fierce gales of our souls. Guardians of the East, we welcome you.

I invoke the powers of the South: by the Fire of life that burns within us, by lightning and lava, by the bonfires and hearths that mark the turning of the Great Wheel. Guardians of the South, we welcome you.

I invoke the powers of the West: by the Waters that cover our planet, the rain from above us and the springs from below, the tears of our ancestors and the blood of our kindred. Guardians of the West, we welcome you.

The circle is cast in love and trust. Reach out to your neighbors and welcome them to the circle in love and trust.

We stand now between the worlds of matter and spirit, beyond the bounds of time, where love and magic are the laws. Here night and day, joy and sorrow, victory and defeat meet and become one, each completing the other. We gather tonight in that time when the curtain between the worlds is sheer, to honor those who have gone before us. In this time of Muin the Vine, we send out tendrils of brightness and love into the darkness, giving our Ancestors a light to guide them back to our hearth. As is right and proper, we follow the ancient laws of hospitality as we welcome to our circle the recently dead and the beloved Long Dead. Some of us believe that at Samhain, the Holy Ones begin the sleep that lasts until Alban Arthan and the Yuletide. We wish them deep sleep and wise dreams, and will tend the sacred fires until their returning.

All: Deep sleep, beloved.

Gather the wise counsel all around you. Listen to the wind in the leaves—it is the voices of the dead. Spend time alone in silence that the mystery may be revealed to you, for the good of self and village and tribe. Fear not, sisters and brothers. Greet the Old Ones, tend their burial places, extend the hand of hospitality, which is their right and is our duty.

Speaking of Names

As a community, we have experienced the passing of many souls this long year. Tonight, in this place of stillness and power, I invite each of you to speak the name of your loved ones who have made that transition from matter to spirit, who have gone to the applelands, to Tir Nan Og. Honor them, mourn their passing as the year darkens, remember their love and brightness.

The names are spoken. When all have spoken:

The word "witch hunt" has become synonymous with the relentless pursuit of an innocent person. I hear it used on the news with increasing frequency, as the roots of our country are shaken again and again through our own actions. But few people who use or hear that word nowadays know its origins in the European Middle Ages, when the theocracies of Europe unleashed the power of the Inquisition on their own people and later carried the contagion into North and South America. We don't know how many died at the hands of the state or the church or at the hands of their neighbors. We do know the methods used—strappado and wheel, noose and stake. We estimate that eighty percent of the victims in Europe were women, from which we get the stereotype of the green-faced crone and her cauldron and her broom. History books rarely discuss it, and history teachers are uncomfortable teaching it. Modern Witches have given this centuries-long horror a name—we call it "the Burning Times." Tonight we remember the victims and we acknowledge the fear. We remember all those who have suffered religious persecution. We remember the countless unnamed dead who yielded up their lives during the Burning Times. There are slips of paper on the altar, paper covered with clear glass stones. Please step forward as you are moved, read a name, and drop the stone into the cauldron. As each stone is placed, I ask the onlookers to take a deep breath as each jewel goes into the water, and hold the memory of that soul for a moment in your hearts.

The names are read.

Silence.

Funerary prayer.

We can hear the music in the mist
The drums that echo our sad hearts.
We can see your bright eyes and your smile.
And so we open the gate
We push back the door
We hold the gate open
We glance through the doorway
Hail the Traveler!
All those remembered in love, in honor,
Live on.
Farewell, O best loved,
O fairest,
Farewell.

The Working

In this deep and sacred place, today we will do a working. I'll guide you through a simple tonal chant designed to raise energy. We will use our collected energy to ease open the portal between the worlds. This is the work we are all called to do during Samhain-tide—to open the door for our nearest and dearest, to welcome them and to hear their words of wisdom and peace.

Chant and Release

There is a place in Ireland called Loughcrew and sometimes the Hill of the Witch. It is a high and windy hill that was used by local tribes for ceremony and burial in Neolithic times. The hill has an intact mound and several other burial chambers. We did ritual there, standing in a burial chamber within a circle of stones. Legend has it that the ancient necropolis was placed on the hilltop so that the people below—the Descendants—could feel the presence and blessing of the Ancestors at all times, that the beloved Long Dead looked down on them lovingly and with great pride.

We stand at a liminal time, where endless possibilities confront us at every turn. I have heard voices whisper behind and around me, voices filled with doubt and fear about the state of affairs on our blessed Earth. As the year darkens and the light dies, we have paths laid before us, and now in spirit we stand at Hekate's crossroad. We may creep together down the path of fear and dread, clutching each other, projecting our growing fear into the enveloping darkness. Or we may straighten our backs and look this fear in the eye and project into this darkness the joy and ecstasy and strength that we desire to find on our own blessed Earth.

I choose this second path. I choose to create the reality I seek. I choose to send my will and the power of my Ancestors and kin into the darkness, to claim my birthright as a child of the Goddess. I invite you to join me on this path of knowledge and ecstasy.

Light the Cauldron Fire/Candle

Because our ancestors trusted that darkness becomes light and that the wheel will always turn, here as the darkness and winter are set to engulf our world, we also celebrate a new year. As the light grows from the center out, let the warmth and light within our hearts turn the wheel into a new year and bless our earth with health and vigor. Blessed be. Happy New Year!
Dismiss the Quarters. Stand as you are able.
Guardians of the West, go if you must, stay if you will.
Repeat for the South, East, and North.
The circle is open but never again broken. Merry meet and merry part and merry meet again.

Benediction

May the unknowable workings of the universe protect you as you go forth tonight. May the solid earth uphold you, the winds of change inspire you, the fire of inspiration ignite within you, and the waters of life nourish you. Go forth in strength and light under this autumn sky. Greet the life-force with joy and gladness from this day until the end of time. Walk in pride and wisdom and love, bringing blessings to yourself, your kin, and all you meet, behaving in such a way that our ancestors will look upon us, their descendants, with pride. For we are all part of the deep and ancient force that flows through all things.
So mote it be, Great Ones. Blessed be.

Berm: Passages

Adoption

Some ceremonies can be left fairly open and work well unformed, allowing the energy and emotion of the event guide the shape and the direction. This ceremony here is for a teenager's adoption into a loving family. They had an idea of what they wanted to say and what they intended in the celebration. I was merely the MC for the event, guiding the process.

Music plays softly throughout. A table is set in the middle of the circle. There is a container for flowers that has pictures of each family member on it with a ribbon tying them together. There are candles.

Family and guests circle up in the backyard.

The outer circle (the guests) are linked together wrist to wrist with yarn.

Welcome.

Officiant welcomes everyone and states the intention/ the reason for the celebration.

The adopted person reads a poem.

The guests are invited to speak about the adopted person and her family.

Parents speak.

Adopted person speaks.

The family gathers around the celebration table at the center of the circle, and they light their individual candles and together light the family candle.

Officiant asks the guests to give their blessings to the family.

Benediction and an invitation to share the joy of the family through the sharing of food.

Graduate School Blessing (for a Student)

Smudge. Anoint. Raise circle.
Student states intention. Bestow gifts.
Officiant: I place the torc of protection upon you. I place the girdle of power upon you. I place the crown of judgment upon you. Walk in grace. Walk in joy. Walk in wisdom. This is your charge.
Draw in and bestow the powers.
Officiant: Wisdom of raven be thine. Clear sight of eagle be thine. Stillness of moon be thine. Power of storm be thine. Goodness of sea be thine. Goodness of earth be thine. And vision of the heavens.

Blessings

Officiant: May each day bring you joy, may no day bring you grief. May you walk with the Goddess on your right hand and on your left hand. Before you and behind you. Above you and below you. Walk a path that leads to wisdom. Walk a path that is itself wisdom. May you walk your path in honor.
Release Quarters and the Circle.

First Blood

This is the celebration of a girl's first menstruation. It is often preceded by the girl in segregation for several hours, when she is instructed by the older women in the group on hygiene, fertility, and safe and joyful sex. Near the time for the ceremony, her body may be painted or otherwise adorned, her hair dressed, and her body massaged with sweet-smelling oils.
The quarters are called, the guardians are welcomed, and the circle is raised.

Consecration

The women are robed and masked, representing the Ancestral Goddesses. They are left wrist to left wrist, in a loose circle of red yarn. The Initiate is brought into the circle blindfolded, and the ordeal begins. The girl is placed in the middle of the circle, and the women are silent.

Finally a single drumbeat slowly begins.

The women ask the following questions.

Who are you? (Birth name, nicknames.)

Why have you come before us?

By what right do you claim the privileges and rights of womanhood?

What is your Mother clan? (Her matrilineal line.)

What now is your name? (Chosen or clan name.)

When the girl has successfully answered these questions, her wrist is bound with that of the last woman in the circle, and the invocation is given.

Invocation

We have within this web of women a new woman. She is our sister _____. She has gone deep to find answers, and she now knows that her soul holds and reveals to her ancient knowledge through the offering of her sacred blood. She knows that all answers can be found within.

Response: Blessed be.

The yarn is cut.

Officiant: Before the Ancestral Goddesses, the guardians and the Ancestors, she has recited the line of her mother clan and claimed her place in the lineage. Her body is no longer a child's body. It is a woman's body with all its joys and terrors, with its freedom and its responsibilities. She bleeds the sacred blood, the lifeblood of our species. Never forget that this is a holy thing, a sign from the Goddess. The blood is our power as creator, destroyer, warrior, queen, woman, virgin, mother, crone.

Response: Blessed be.

Officiant: Behold this powerful and glorious woman. Because she is strong, she bleeds but does not die. She sacrifices her blood for the good of her people. She draws from earth, air, fire, and water and creates within her womb the sacred elemental blood.

Response: Blessed be.

The blindfold is removed.

Response: You were born naked from your mother's womb.

New woman: Blessed be.

Officiant: You stand before the mothers adorned and bare, as is right. Bare as a newborn child is bare, yet adorned with the jewel of your new womanhood. But it is also proper for a new woman, a new goddess, to be adorned in beautiful things.

The women come forward and dress the new woman in her ritual garments. Her mother crowns her with a flower crown. The foster mother steps to the new woman's side, carrying the athame or other rituals tools.

The mother speaks: I am _____. I stand with my daughter on the day of her naming. This woman is the child of my womb, my companion on the path of the ancestors and the beloved Long Dead. Who else stands with her?

Foster mother: I am_____. This woman is the child of my soul, my companion on the path. I stand as her foster mother and her friend.

Companion: I am _____. This woman is the sister of my soul, my companion on the path. I stand as her Goddess-sister and her friend.

Mother: I am satisfied that _____is prepared to step through this gateway.

Foster mother: I am satisfied that _____is prepared to step through this gateway.

Companion: I am satisfied that _____is prepared to step through this gateway.

Presentation of the New Woman.

Officiant: This is the token that you are acknowledged as a woman in this circle and within this clan. This blade is not only a symbol of your power and will, it is a magical tool. Keep it sharp. Use it well.

The new woman puts on her jewelry and takes up her magical tools.

Here is our sister _____. Greet this woman and welcome her to this circle of women.

The Ancestral Goddesses remove their masks, and the new woman goes to each in turn, and they speak her name and welcome her. Small gifts, advice, inspiration may be given.

We stand now, woman to woman, at the center of the circle where all things meet their opposites. Take this charm of the silver crescent as a reminder of this. As the horned moon represents the Goddess's giver of life, so also does it symbolize the horns of the Queen of Death; she who has the power to create life also has the power to take it.

Inanna and Erishkegal.

Durga and Kali.

Demeter and Persephone.

Brigid and the Morrighan.

To step through this portal into womanhood is to accept this responsibility.

Benediction and Final Blessing

The new woman's forehead is smeared with ocher.

I bless you with the blessings of the Goddess. I send you forth marked with Her sign that all who meet you may know Her.

Remember always that you are Her child. She is with you always. Do nothing to shame Her—or yourself.

The guardians are thanked and the circle is opened.

Here's a ritual at the other end of the menstrual process. I have facilitated it for several years at the Southeast Wise Woman Herbal Conference.

The Ceremony of Croning

Casting the Spiral.

Here is the Mystery.

Thus is the Spiral set—

Four elemental goddesses hold the sacred precinct.

Three quarters are Earth and Air and Fire,

with the Womblike Waters holding the Center.

Two then are You and She.

One is the Center, the Union of All That Is.

Spiral in, spiral out.

Thus is our spiral set.

I cast this circle in stone and steel. Guardians and Ancestors in the North! Be welcome to this circle and stand here with your kindred. We, your people, honor you. So mote it be.

I cast this circle in stone and steel. Guardians and Ancestors in the East! Be welcome to this circle, and stand here with your kindred. We, your people, honor you. So mote it be.

I cast this circle in stone and steel. Guardians and Ancestors in the South! Be welcome to this circle and stand here with your kindred. We, your people, honor you. So mote it be.

I cast this circle in stone and steel. Guardians and Ancestors in the West! Be welcome to this circle and stand here with your kindred. We, your people, honor you. So mote it be.

And now do we call to our shoulders those Crones of Winter whose bones are ice, whose breath is mist, whose heart is iron.

Welcome and Intention Setting

What is a Crone? The phases of Woman—child, maiden, free spirit, mother, warrior, queen, crone, hag.

All: Invocation by breathing Her name

Cailleach.

Baba Yaga.

Hekate.

Naming of New Crone/s. The gathered women speak their new names, if they have taken one.

Blessing of the Elements

In a small group you can do these one by one. In a larger group, you may choose to do it once for everyone.

May the blessings of Earth be upon this good woman in her crone years. Grant to her your gifts of stability, strength, and prosperity.

Those in attendance say: In abundance!

May the blessings of Air be upon this good woman in her crone years. Grant to her your gifts of wisdom and understanding.

Those in attendance say: In abundance!

May the blessings of Fire be upon this good woman in her crone years. Grant to her your gifts of love, passion, and creativity.

Those in attendance say: In abundance!

May the blessings of Water be upon this good woman in her crone years. Grant to her your gifts of intuition, inspiration, and flexibility.

Those in attendance say: In abundance!

Crone pledges (vows).

Crone/s seated in authority. Words of honor, love, and respect are spoken. Each speaker sits on a small stool or pillow at the crone's feet.

Crone Wisdom. Words from the new Crone/s.

From Kate O'Connor:

Crone Song

> *then i was taut: a bowstring*
> *quivering in anticipation of flight.*
> *i have become grounded—*
> *porous and yielding.*
> *i bend with the movement;*
> *the now... the past...*
> *the future...*
> *all present in the same soil.*
> *then i shot fast and blazing true*
> *toward the eye of the sun—*
> *blurred the line*
> *between heaven and earth.*
> *in these measured days*
> *i shade my face;*
> *stoop to slowly stroke*
> *the fragile fallen leaves*
> *that hug the loam*
> *preparing to fade and*
> *dissolve*

to feed tomorrow's blooms
from deep below.

Circle weaving dance. Crone/s lead a simple circle dance; drums here.
Words of gratitude.
Unwinding Spiral.

The spiral stretches.
The uncoiling begins.
Life! Mystery!
One becomes Two,
You and She,
Becomes the Earth and all she contains.
Four Elemental Goddesses share the power
and the wealth
and the wisdom.
Here is the Mystery as
The spiral releases,
Unfurling into the universe.
Becoming the All.

BERM: ORDINATION

Sometimes we act as priestess or priest to our families only, but some people are called to serve as clergy for a community or a house of worship. Here is an ordination ritual from Mother Grove Goddess Temple.

I was asked to participate in the ordination ritual of an Earth-focused Christian church. I was asked to speak to the ordinand from the place of a community leader. What follows was my warning to him.

We all come from the Goddess. And to Her we shall return—like a drop of rain, flowing to the ocean.

The Divines take ordination very seriously. It has been my experience that there is a brief honeymoon period following the ceremony of ordination and then they—in their infinite wisdom—will test you. We all think we've been tested—had our trials and tribulations. And if we're blessed, we've learned strong lessons. But when your heart pledges service, they need for you to be sure, to know what you're getting into and so... a test, just like in the ancient tales. Remember that we stand with you, they love you, and the world needs you.

One of the ways to thrive in the testing is through listening—to them, to your heart, to your community, to the Earth and your Ancestors. Real listening begins in a hard place—hearing things you don't want to hear, deep listening without frantically trying to fix things, lingering in the mystery.

We have so much work to do, you know. The brokenness of the culture can only be mended, I suspect, by those of us who have been broken by it and somehow glued the bits together enough to stand upright, lock arms with our kindred, and stumble forward, dancing.

All acts of love and pleasure are Her rituals. Blessed be your service and your vows, my brother. Blessed be you. And blessed be we.

The Rite of Ordination

During setup, ordinands create the altar and call in their Matrons. Then they go upstairs to wait.
Ingathering (recorded music).
Charge of the Goddess is read.
Song (We are blessed to sometimes have the services of the Sahara Peace choir, and its leader and songsmith Annelinde Metzner).
Welcome.
Raise the Circle with singing bowl.

Setting the Intention for the evening, letting the congregation know that the priestesses will enter during this song.

Song: "Sahara Peace Choir."

Priestesses enter during song; priestesses are seated.

What is a priestess? An experienced priestess shares her experience

The ordinands' personal cords are tied.

Song: "Sahara Peace Choir."

What is a priestess? Another experienced priestess shares her reflections.

Tying on Mother Grove cords.

Vows: personal.

Vows: corporate.

Their stoles are draped around their shoulders.

Blessing of the priestesses: the congregation blesses and empowers their new clergy.

The new clergy open the circle and bless the congregation.

Drumming (or recorded music) as the group moves to the reception.

Here is a second ritual that is simpler since only one ordinand was being elevated.
- Rite of Ordination
- Mother Grove Goddess Temple
- Ingathering
- Song
- The Charge of the Goddess
- Welcome
- Circle Cast
- Set Intention
- Song: "Oya, You are the Wind!"
- Invocation of Oya
- The clergy invoke their Matrons

- Ordinand enters
- What is a priestess?
- Presentation of cords
- Song, as Ordinand ties her cords
- Poem
- Speaking the Vows
- Renewal of Vows, by clergy
- Presentation of Stole
- Blessing of the Sisters—with honey (that your service be sweet), with wine (that you always deepen your connection to the mystery), with bread (that your ministry nourish and sustain you).
- Blessing of the Congregation—all sing "Ode to Joy."
- Ordinand returns to clergy to be empowered—congregation tones, singing bowl is rung.
- Presentation of New Clergy
- Circle is opened
- New clergy blesses the congregation
- Reception follows

BERM: SEASONAL

Among the Fields of Gold

Fill the altar with the following: corn, wheat, corn dollies, Harvest Goddess, bread, oats, barley, squash, sickle/reap hook, Appalachian hand pictures, bread, apple juice, oats, kamut, grinder, broom.

Sweep the area.

Assign two people as gatekeepers.

Smudge/anoint.

Welcome/housekeeping: bathroom, food, sign up for temple emails, phones off, introduce ourselves and helpers.

Circle up.

Announcement of temple:

Friends, the temple is about to be erected and the circle cast. Let those who desire attendance gather now to prepare our sacred space. Let none be here but of their own free will.

Cast the circle: I conjure here a circle of power, a sacred and intentional space for worship and celebration, a meeting place of joy and love and truth, a boundary between the world of humanity and the realms of the shining ones.

With steel I set a guardian and protection that shall preserve and contain the power that we shall raise within thee. This I will, in the name of the people. Wherefore do I consecrate this temple in the name of great Tailtiu and of our own Tahkeeostee and beloved Tonatzin. May we all blessed be.

Cast.

North: In this time of the grain harvest, I call the Ancestors and the Guardians of the North with the strength of oats! I remember how the seed heads, tanned from the sun, stand in the wide fields near the river. I remember the threshing of the grain and the stretching stomachs it fills. I remember the bowl, with butter and sugar, and a man dressed as a friend. Hail and welcome to our table!

East: In this time of the grain harvest, I call the Ancestors and Guardians of the East with the bright yellow kernels of corn! I have planted the flat kernels in mounds the width of my hand. I have seen the shocking green of the stalks as they rise. The oldest peoples put a fish's head in the mound to feed the proud, tall spears that hold the other sister. Hail and welcome to our table!

South: In this time of the grain harvest, I call the Ancestors and Guardians of the South with the banked fire of wheat! I sing now of the fire of the sun, of the loaf made edible through the flailing of the grain. I sing now of the bright fire of food that is enduring, of food that is beautiful to see. I sing of grains that feed the people and straw that makes the bricks. Hail and welcome to our table!

West: In this time of the grain harvest, I call the Ancestors and Guardians of the West with the perfect jewels of barley! I create a necklace of the pearls of barley. I create soup from the waters of the sea and the tears of my kindred, who passed into the West. I create the living vision of a shining new world. I create a passageway for my descendants to greet my ancestors. Hail and welcome to our table!

Center, Invocation of Tailtiu

> *Go raibh maith agat*
> *do fomhar, do baisteach, do gra.*

And so our circle is cast.

Temple talk, explain ritual.

What have you cleared with brute strength? When have you done something the hard way? Why?

Officiant: Famine in the world and call for sacred fast day; the story of Tailtiu.

Appalachian women/grannies who were broken to clear the land/women who did it all; bread for your people.

Cakes and ale.

Around circle widdershins with sword.

Opening the circle: Go with thanks and go with blessing, Sweet Lady of the gardens, Lady of the pastures, Lady of the orchards. Or stay, for you are in our hearts always.

West: Sweet pearls, rich grain. Barley of my people. Though our circle be open, we honor the West! Blessed Grandmothers, e'er you depart for your sweet and blessed realms, we bid you hail and farewell!

South: Bread-maker, brick-maker: wheat of the plains. Though our circle be open, we honor the South! Beloved Grandmothers, e'er you depart for your sweet and blessed realms, we bid you hail and farewell!

East: The tall sister, the one who stands, silk and husk of corn. Though our circle be open, we honor the East! Beloved Grandmothers, e'er you depart for your sweet and blessed realms, we bid you hail and farewell!

North: Tanned for the harvest, sweet beyond measure. Oats for our bellies. Though our circle be open, we honor the North! Beloved Grandmothers, e'er you depart for your sweet and blessed realms, we bid you hail and farewell!

The circle is open but never again broken. May the Goddess fill all hearts as the grains of autumn come to harvest. Merry meet and merry part! And merry meet again!

Beltane: Welcoming the Summer Maiden

Maidens to anoint (anoint with sprinkling branch). People enter the circle through Baba Yaga's flower hoops as a symbol of rebirth.

We raise a traditional circle.

North: (with drumming) We'll begin in the North with the great greenness of the land in summer. (Drumming commences.) Feel that heartbeat? It is the land living within us and around us. Feel your own heartbeat now and come into the great rhythm of the land in summer—fertile, luscious, green of lichen and fern, tree and moss. Spirits of this land, our land, we honor and welcome you. (Drumming ceases.) Blessed be.

East: (with whistle) Turn with me now to the East and the sweet scent of summer. (Whistle commences.) Breathe deeply of this scent of summer. There is river in it and composting leaves from last year's autumn. Take in the richness of the tree breath, and join our elder kindred in welcoming the sun and the warm and the winds of change. Spirits of this air, our air, we honor and welcome you. (Whistle ceases.) Blessed be.

South: (with rattle) Let's face the South now and raise up the great bonfires of the season. (Rattling commences.) Put your hand on your brow. Do you feel the heat that is you, the fire that courses through your blood? Close your eyes and feel the reflection of the great bonfires of old, flickering against your eyes. Welcome in the heat of summer. Spirits of this fire, our fire, we honor and welcome you. (Rattling ceases.) Blessed be.

West: (with singing bowl) We end our cast facing the West and calling in the summer rains. (Singing bowl commences.) We stand so near our old river—do you feel her, restless, moving northward? Do you feel the sweat on your face, the moisture in your mouth? As the summer stretches her long limbs, we hope the gentle rains remember how welcome they are. Spirits of this water, our water, we honor and welcome you. (Singing bowl ceases.) Blessed be. Come back around to the North to make our circle whole.

Maidens skip around the circle to raise it as the Baba Yaga stands in the center, invoked and welcomed.

Invocation of summer with trance posture and chant, ends with and the summer is come.

Ground the energy; center; focus.

Hugs and merry meet.

Setting intention.

The Baba Yaga hands the flower rings over to the Maidens and is farewelled with flower petals, bubbles, singing bowl. She exits the circle.

Circle dance with Maidens leading.

Offering to land spirits and river by the young men for abundant harvest.

Song: "Morning Has Broken."

Cakes and ale.

Sacred dance.

Open circle as in cast.

Quarter Releases

West: (Singing bowl starts it) And now our revels are ended and we honor the Ancestors and Grandmothers of the West. Rain and river and sweet Maywine—go if you must but stay if you will! Blessed be.

South: (Rattle starts it.) And now our revels are ended and we honor the Ancestors and Grandmothers of the South. Bonfire and hearth fire and loving life-force— go if you must but stay if you will! Blessed be.

East: (Whistle starts it.) And now our revels are ended and we honor the Ancestors and Grandmothers of the East. Song and wind and spirits of change— go if you must but stay if you will! Blessed be.

North: (Drumming starts it.) And now our revels are ended and we honor the Ancestors and Grandmothers of the North. Deep green, warm soil, heartbeat of life— go if you must but stay if you will! Blessed be.

Officiant: After our traditional ending, we invite you each to jump through our ring of fire and into the summer country (with drumming).

Exit circle, dancing and leaping through an archway of fabric flames and into the summer country (with music).

A Breath of Appalachian Spring: a Vernal Equinox Celebration

Set up a central altar with balloons, pinwheels, kites, whistles, statue of Laksmi, bright colored cloths.
Set up a side altar of paper for airplanes, pens and pencils.
Set up a second side altar of a candle-lighting table.
Announcements.
Temple talk.
Housekeeping: bathrooms, who we are, turn off phones, thanks to the venue.
Smudge and anoint.
Welcome.
Tell congregants about their response parts.

Invocation of Directions

One officiant speaks, the other whistles. The roles are alternated at each Quarter.
Officiant: I start my calling with the dawn and the East. Mother of sweet breezes and daily inspiration, blow away the cobwebs and the dust bunnies sacred to the season. Keep me light enough to jump and heavy enough to plant the radishes. Sweet jumping eastern mamas, we welcome you here. Right now! (Congregants repeat "Right now!")
Speaking/whistling
Officiant: I keep on calling by turning to the South and the smoke of spring clearings in the garden, careful smoke, cleansing smoke. Mother of applewood smoke,

blow past my twitching nose as I dream the tomatoes that are to come. Sharp, careful, corn-likker-still mamas, we welcome you here. Right now!

(Congregants repeat "Right Now!")

Speaking/whistling

Officiant: I keep on calling by turning to the West and cool wind, bringing spring rains. Off we go, living water that is not frozen. We want to walk in it and feel the drops sprinkling off the trees, the mothers of fruit and flower. Blue-barrel water-toting mamas, we welcome you here. Right now! (Congregants repeat "Right Now!")

Speaking/whistling

Officiant: I finish up calling for now by turning to the North and the smell of good, rich earth. Birdfolks and snakefolks and worms are there, and moles and groundhogs that will eat every tender green thing in your garden. Huh! Mamas with dirty hands and smiling faces, we welcome you here. Right now! (Congregants repeat "Right Now!")

Invocation of Laksmi

> *Salutations to the great enchantress, Laksmi,*
> *The Goddess of wealth,*
> *Who is worshipped by the Devas,*
> *And who holds conch, wheel and mace in her hands.*
> *Again salutations to the Mahalakshmi*
> *To she who wears supreme happiness as ornament.*
> *The Goddess Lakshmi is attracted,*
> *As the black bees are attracted,*
> *To the unopened buds of black Tamala tree,*
> *Let She who is the Goddess of all good things,*
> *Grant us a glance that will bring prosperity.*

Invite participants to sit down.

Ritual Intention. Air-focused, honoring the inner child, spring cleaning, breath of spring, welcome all to a place that is happy and joyous and full of new life.

This ended up being one of our most controversial rituals. We invited the attendees to take a piece of paper and write on it their prayers or wishes for the summer season. Then they shaped those sheets into paper airplanes and spent several minutes flying them around the room, laughing, jumping. They were asked to pick up the airplane nearest them, take the prayer home, and pray someone else's prayer or repeat their intention or wish, for seven days. Observers found this to be a very odd way to celebrate our spirituality.

Cakes and Ale.

Thanking the Goddess/Closing Prayer.

Devocation of Directions: Invite congregants to repeat "Right now."

North: We appreciate your presence and your love and your magic—sweet earthy mamas, the time is now! Right now! (Congregants repeat.)

West: We appreciate your presence and your love and your magic—sweet rainy mamas, the time is now! Right now! (Congregants repeat.)

South: We appreciate your presence and your love and your magic—sweet smoky mamas, the time is now! Right now! (Congregants repeat.)

East: We appreciate your presence and your love and your magic—sweet breezy mamas, the time is now! Right now! (Congregants repeat.)

Crowning the Cailleach: a Winter Solstice Celebration

The following ritual borrows some trappings from more formally structured rites, in both shape and language.

Smudge and anoint.

Participants enter the temple.

Charge of the Goddess. All assembled. Make copies available.

Officiant: (Raise circle with sword). I conjure here a circle of power, a shield against evil, a boundary between the worlds of Earth and ether, a rampart and protection that shall preserve and contain the power that we shall raise within. I bless and consecrate this circle, in the name of the Elder Ones.

Officiant: (Raise circle with stone). I conjure here a circle of power, a shield against evil, a boundary between the worlds of Earth and ether, a rampart and protection that shall preserve and contain the power that we shall raise within. I bless and consecrate this circle, in the name of the Elder Ones.

Officiant: Guardians of the Watchtowers of the East, creatures of air and dawning! I do summon, stir, and call you forth, to be present in our rite and guard our circle. (Draw the Invoking Pentagram.)

Officiant: Guardians of the Watchtowers of the South, creatures of fire and yearning! I do summon, stir, and call you forth, to be present in our rite and guard our circle. (Draw the Invoking Pentagram.)

Officiant: Guardians of the Watchtowers of the West, creatures of water and change! I do summon, stir, and call you forth, to be present in our rite and guard our circle. (Draw the Invoking Pentagram.)

Officiant: Guardians of the Watchtowers of the North, creatures of earth and deep power! I do summon, stir, and call you forth, to be present in our rite and guard our circle. (Draw the Invoking Pentagram.)

Invoke the Cailleach.

First officiant: Last night I felt her stirring. Her chill breath crept cunningly through the screen of the open window, reminding me of the now sudden quieting of the night sounds. I raised the blankets around me to avoid Her touch, but still Her caress found my face. I groaned with the knowledge that She is coming, that She must come. The wheel is turning. I did not see Her face, for I only felt Her stirring. But I am certain it is as the cold blackness of the winter night and the empty stillness of the tomb. I did not meet Her gaze; Her single shining eye that pierces the simplicity of our wonderings and the duplicity of our strivings. Her unyielding gaze has seen the beginnings and the endings of countless lives and seasons. She is the soul-holder, the decider, the finisher of fields and the keeper of the final harvest. She is the ancient earth herself, and those who must will go to Her when soon She brings the winter tempests. Fear Her or fear Her not, for still She will come.

Second officiant: Soon She will be among us. Her breath flows even now as a sigh from the ridgetops; a chill in the early evening sky stirring brittle leaves and rushing the frail ones to their burrows and nests. Her fearsome face peers out between the dying stalks and the crumbling grass. She is the ruler of the paler sun and the freezing times. She carries the deadfall of winter in Her hair. She is the womb of the earth at rest. She is the Ancestress of our Ancestors veiled by the passage of time.

Fear Her or fear Her not, for still She comes.

Both officiants: You are coming. We welcome you, the Cailleach, the Winter Queen.

(A curtain is pulled back to reveal the Winter Queen and attendants.)

Officiant: Cailleach means old woman. Bheur is sharp. The Cailleach Bheur is the ancient Queen of Winter, possibly the eldest Goddess of the British Isles. She has been worn down over the centuries from deity to giantess, from giantess to the archetypal witch. Her name now is Gaelic, but it seems She was there from ages before, waiting for them to come and call her Crone.

Second officiant: The wizened old hag goddesses appear closely linked to particular locations throughout the British Isles. The Cailleach is not a national deity of a whole country but is rather bound closely to the land associated with particular mountains, rivers, lochs, and other wild places. Her form—the powerful old giantess—may be almost identical wherever She appears, but Her name and Her tales are localized.

Officiant: We invoke Her now as Pisgah and Mitchell, as Swannanoa and Tahkeostee. Her fruits are the pomegranate and the apple. We invite each of you now to spend a moment with the Winter Queen and to leave any burdens you do not wish to carry through the dark months. Pour a little pomegranate juice over Her stone, saying "I let go of _____ and leave it in the lap of the Hag."

Take a gift from the Hag, candy from Her lap/altar.

Officiant: Guardians of the Watchtowers of the North, creatures of Earth, guardians of the northern portal, we do thank you for attending these honorable rites. Ere you depart to your pleasant and lovely realms, we bid you hail and farewell! (Make the banishing pentacle.)

Officiant: Guardians of the Watchtowers of the West, creatures of Water, guardians of the western portal, we do thank you for attending these honorable rites. Ere you depart to your pleasant and lovely realms, we bid you hail and farewell! (Make the banishing pentacle.)

Officiant: Guardians of the Watchtowers of the South, creatures of Fire, guardians of the southern portal, we do thank you for attending these honorable rites. Ere you depart to your pleasant and lovely realms, we bid you hail and farewell! (Make the banishing pentacle.)

Officiant: Guardians of the Watchtowers of the East, creatures of Air, guardians of the eastern portal, we do thank you for attending these honorable rites. Ere you depart to your pleasant and lovely realms, we bid you hail and farewell! (Make the banishing pentacle.)

All: Our circle is open but never again broken. Merry meet and merry part and merry meet again.

Sometimes we are silly, intentionally. Anointing with mustard as we did in the following ritual is not something I'd recommend nor do again.

Midsummer Madness

S'mores and ice water for cakes and ale.
Smudge and anoint with hibachi and mustard.
Set up your altar honoring the tikis, leis, etc.
Ingathering.
Announcements: welcome, housekeeping, donations, memberships, Thirteenth Circle.
Smudge and anoint.
Raise the circle.
Invoke the Goddess/s.
North: We call to the fertile valleys and hills of the North country, and we honor summer's fire in the magic of charcoal. Behold! Wood that is burned slowly, slowly—and still burns again to roast our corn. Let us always honor the gift of the trees that give us charcoal. Hail and be welcome to midsummer!
East: We call to the bright sun as it dawns in the midsummer sky. Behold! This longest day is decorated and illuminated and our skins scorched by the blinding glow of the summer sun. Let us honor the sun with dark glasses, sunscreen, and whoops of joy! Hail and be welcome to midsummer!
South: We call to the burning light of the South, and we honor the child of the charcoal—the grilling fire. Behold! We spread the coals and light them with skill, and the glow and heat cooks hotdog, veggie burger, and the sacred s'mores. Let us honor the fire with care and delight. Hail and be welcome to midsummer!
West: We call to the waves on the beaches of the West and honor the critters that live in tidal ponds. Behold! There are little crabs in the water and barnacles that cling to the rocks. We cool our feet and wet our swimsuits in the squishy sand of the tidal ponds. Let

us honor the water with splashes of delight! Hail and welcome to midsummer!

We call out to the bounty of the great round Earth, and we invoke the Triple Goddess of Picnic Sides. All hail, the Maiden in Her form as sweet and ripe watermelon, sacred to Erzulie and Yemaya. All hail, the Mother in Her form as rich baked beans—tangy and filling, sacred to Selu and Roman Carna. All hail, the Crone in Her form as perfect potato salad—the assembling of all wisdom, with celery and mayonnaise. And be welcome the attendants—devilled eggs, chips, pickles, and corn on the cob. We welcome you to this, our midsummer celebration.

And so our circle is cast.

Intention, focus our strengths. Officiant asks participants to talk about their strengths, then reverse and name their weaknesses. Energy is raised through chant as we transform our weakness into strength and throw the weakness into the river.

Cakes and ale.

Open circle and devoke goddesses.

All participants walk to the river and return singing "The River is Flowing."

A blessing is said over the potluck that follows the ritual.

A Rose in Winter: Winter Solstice with Mother Grove

Smudge and Anoint.

Start in low light.

Welcome and housekeeping (phones, bathrooms, donation, food pantry—collection points, taking food, big thanks to the venue).

Raise circle.

Officiant: Here at the gateway of the year, may we strive to make good cheer. In our revels shall joy abound and sorrow be cast underground!

North: In winter, the forest is still and deep. The hearts of the trees beat slowly, the bears dream of blueberries and fierce love. Stones are cold, blades of grass sharp as steel. In winter, the forest is still.

East: In winter, our breath makes clouds in the chill day. Sunrise comes too early, and sunset does the same. Ankle winds force us into stout boots, and we wrap our faces against the night. In winter, our breath makes clouds.

South: In winter, we warm our hands at the fire. Mantles over fireplaces hold fragrant and evergreen branches, hold stockings at Yuletide. Bonfires reach skyward, and candles hold promises. In winter, we warm our hands at the fire.

West: In winter, water is slippery stone. Icicles line the window ledges, jagged teeth. Water, soft and beautiful, falls white upon the fields and beaches. And the sea, eternal, caresses Her dancing tides. In winter, water is slippery stone.

Officiant: Let the harp of the new moon sound and mark our celebration! Omnia tempus habent! (There is time for everything!)

Invocation of Divine. Priestess leads us in "O Holy Night."

Poem "Dawning of Solstice" by Dorothy Morrison.

Instruct participants about the solstice, Saturnalia, Christmas, shortest night, Sol Invictus.

Officiant: We talk so much about community and resilience and the changes that are rolling over and through us right now. In a few minutes, we will all celebrate the Ceremony of Cakes and Ale, which is our promise to each other. We promise to stick together, to have each other's backs, to share our bounty, to hold a space for wonder and for mystery. This poem, by Goodwyn Barmby, was published in 1851 and still holds a way to model the community we wish so much to become.

Priestess recites poem as follows:

This Is Now The Wintertime

This is now the winter time
My merry neighbors
Yule logs are burning in your hall
Fair forms are circling in the ball
And cups are filled with purple wine
To aid the pudding and the chine
This is now the winter time
Remember gentle neighbors
That none shall starve while you dine
That none shall thirst that grow the vine
Yet give no alms in mean award
But spread the just, well-earned board
This is now the winter time
My noble neighbors.

The Ceremony of Cakes and Ale: apple juice and gingerbread.

Teaching.

Priestess introduces tradition of giving gifts and explains the working. Clementines are passed out and instructions to confer a blessing on the person to the left and give the clementine as a gift.

Read "The Shortest Day" by Susan Cooper.

One of the priestesses explains that the main altar's candles will be lighted and then the light moves out, into the gathered folks.

All: Chanting/stomping/ringing bells to welcome back the sun.

Carol/Song.

Priestess leads a simple clockwise circle dance while singing "Deck the Halls."

Open the Circle.

West: Snow and icicle. Black ice and Brigid spring. Water like stone. Water like stone. Blessed be Water and blessed be all we. Happy solstice!

South: Bonfire. Hearthfire. Candle and incense. Bonfires reach skyward. Bonfires reach skyward. Blessed be Fire and blessed be all we. Happy solstice!

East: Clouds of breath. Early dawning. Wrapped against the winds and chill. Breath like clouds. Breath like clouds. Blessed be Air and blessed be all we. Happy solstice!

North: Tree and stone. Sharp cold grass and dreams of blueberries. The forest is still. The forest is still. Blessed be the Earth and blessed be all we. Happy solstice!

Blessing for the Road and the Season

So many of us have mourned and worried throughout this past year. I've heard so many express the wish that 2017 be done and good riddance. Take a moment now, before we dance our way into the unknown future, to think on the lessons you have learned. Think of the people you have said farewell to and the baggage you will leave at the threshold of this new time. Blessed be the fine old world, blessed be the peoples who call it home, blessed be our ancestors, and blessed be we.

Please turn to your neighbor and bless them in the old traditional way—blessed be!

Wassail, friends! Good health and prosperity in the new year!

Clergy team sings the following:

Wassail, wassail, all over the town!
Our toast it is white and our ale it is brown.
Our bowl it is made from the red maple tree.
With the wassailing bowl, we drink unto thee!

Merry part. Our circle is open but never again broken!
May the Goddess awaken in every heart!
Merry meet, and merry part
And merry meet again!
Good Yule! Happy Solstice! Sol Invicta!

Earth Day Ritual: The Dirt Worshippers' Ball

We added Earth Day as a holy day, making it part of the Wheel of the Year (Quarter and Cross-Quarter days). Here's an example of one of our Earth Day celebrations. This was originally presented as the main ritual at Blue Ridge Beltane, in Virginia.

Officiant: That smell of soft rain on fresh soil... the feel of grass on bare feet. As Folk of the Earth, we celebrate Beltane in earthy ways—gardening, dancing, walking in the hills, singing with our chosen family, loving those we love. In this ritual, we will come into deep relationship with the ancient highlands as we weave this community into a strong, sustainable basket. Chant, dance, guided meditation and intentional communion guide us into a place of bliss and beautiful connection, of power and action. This ritual is suitable for all ages and abilities. Come set the manifesto for dirty dancing and wild resilience at the Dirt Worshippers' Ball!

Circle up.

Officiant: welcome/housekeeping, phones off, introductions, thank you to venue, anointing.

Call Quarters.

North: I honor the North through the marvelous earthworm. Blind and hopeful, moving through the dark and moist of the world, always searching, always finding. Making soil through your castings, you are humble, elegant, perfect, the garden's friend, the birds' delight. You fling yourself, little cousin, onto the asphalt pathways, avoiding the new rain—drawn up from your perfect tunnels into the air and the light of the sky. Welcome, earthworms!

East: I honor the East through the power of dirt. What is better in all the world than the smell of earth as it begins to rain? How can we love this stuff enough? We use it up, we make it, we ignore it, we adore it. It's under our nails and on our feet; it is the very ground of all existence. Rich, loamy, friable, precious, microbe-filled, the brown skirt of our oldest kin, wide and welcome grandmother. Welcome, dirt!

South: I honor the South through the fickleness of rain. Come back, little sister, when the parched land pines for you. The rivers are longing for presence, the old apple trees shed their green fruit when you play hard-to-get. We love your light touch, your blessing, even your faithlessness. Splash, little sister, through our lives, making us puddles of summer glory. Welcome, rain!

West: I honor the West through the infinity of seeds. We were all seeds once. So were trees and beets and corn. Those little crusty bits of life, the little mothers. You are the multitude of beginnings. We cast you forth, to the wind and the earth and the rain and to life. Burrow your hard self into the bosom of our dear mother and bring forth all that we are, all that we need, all that we dream. Large in possibility, small in size. We welcome seeds!

All: Welcome, sweet Beltane!

Spiral Cast.

Here is the Mystery.
Thus is the spiral set.
Four elemental Goddesses hold the sacred precinct.
Three quarters are Earth and Air and Fire,
with the Womblike Waters holding the Center.
Two then are You and She.
One is the Center,
the Union of All That Is.
Spiral in, spiral out.
Thus is our spiral set.

Teach about the season, community, and Beltane.

Chant—Oak and Ash and Thorn.

Attendees jump the broom to take a leap of faith into community, then dance the Circassian dance or a spiral dance.

Unwind Spiral Cast.

The spiral stretches.
The uncoiling begins.
Life! Mystery!
One becomes Two,
You and She,
Becomes the Earth and all she contains.
Four Elemental Goddesses share the power
and the wealth and the wisdom.
Here is the Mystery as the spiral releases,
Unfurling into the universe.
Becoming the All.

Devocation of the Directions

West: Little mothers on the wind and in the soil, clutched in the fur of the cat, blown by a child from the head of a spent weed. Remain with us as a blessing, if you will. Leave us to travel with your bounty over the whole of the dear earth, if you must. Blessed be!

South: Little sister, call our names! Speak to us on the tin roof and in the rain barrel, as you drip from the branches above. We love your going, and we love your arrival. Stay for a while and then go your ways, as if we can tell you what to do. Blessed be!

East: We want you to stay and not fly away on the dry wind, not flow in mud down embankments to silt up the creeks. Stay in your thickness and richness and if you must go, let us share you with our neighbors as bags of black gold, the most precious thing on earth. Blessed be!

North: Little cousins, be with us always. Let us find you in the garden and under the compost. But go where you must, doing what you do, knowing our love and respect go with you. Blessed be!

Open the Circle

Now by the Earth that is Her body, by the Air that is Her breath, by the Fire of Her bright spirit and the living Waters of Her womb, this circle is open but yet unbroken. May the Goddess awaken in our hearts. Merry meet and merry part and merry meet again!

May this season of Beltane bless you with strongest desires well met, with delicious encounters well times, with space for love and play and lust and passion. May you taste sweetness and softness, firm flesh of peach— and of lover. Blessed be the season and the summer and blessed be all we.

Happy Beltane! Turn to your neighbor now and wish them the joys of the season.

Ring Out Solstice Bells!

Smudge and anoint. Bee-smoker does smudging, anoints. Participants receive Chanukah candles.
Raise the Circle while ringing bells.
North: Please turn with me to the North. We are standing, standing on the blue ball of the green Earth. We are standing, standing on an ancient world, with Ancestors and spirits all around us. We are standing, standing on a precious planet spinning silently in time. Blessed be our planet and blessed be all who are her children. Response: Blessed be!
East: Please turn with me to the East. We are loving, loving the sun in its returning. We are loving, loving the distant lights so filled with stories, the Big Dipper, Orion's Belt. We are loving, loving the stars in the midnight dome above us. Blessed be our star, our sweet sun and blessed be all who are sing it home. Response: Blessed be!
South: Please turn with me to the South. We are following, following the visitors from far away. We are following, following the tails of these swift travelers in their going. We are following, following the legends of their passing, the names we can't pronounce. Blessed be the comets in their flight and blessed be all who watch for them. Response: Blessed be!
West: Please turn with me to the West. We are dreaming, dreaming of her ever-changing face. We are dreaming, dreaming of the tides in their yearning, the cycles of the days. We are dreaming, dreaming of the moon in her fullness, in her darkness, in her glory. Blessed be the moon and blessed be her children. Response: Blessed be!
Charge of the Goddess.

Welcome and housekeeping: turn off phones, leave a donation of food or money, take food if you need it, our thanks for the use of the venue.

Solstice teaching.

Officiant lights the main altar, and then the light moves out into the gathered folks.

Officiant leads a carol or song, and participants do a simple clockwise circle dance while singing "Deck the Halls."

All participate in chanting/stomping/ringing bells to welcome back the sun.

The Ceremony of Cakes and Ale.

Introduction by priestess: Find your match. Each person is given a gold chocolate coin with a number on it. They spend some time finding their match and wishing them a good solstice.

Song: "Holly and the Ivy."

Song: "In the Bleak Midwinter," first verse.

Finish with wishing each other all joys of the season.

Release the quarters.

West: First the West. Dreaming, we say farewell. Dreaming, we hold you close forever. Blessed be the West and the moon.

South: And now the South. Following, we say farewell. Following, we hold you close forever. Blessed be the South and the comets.

East: East is next. Loving, we say farewell. Loving, we hold you close forever. Blessed be the East and the undying sun.

North: We end where we began—in the North. Standing, we say farewell. Standing, we hold you close forever. Blessed be the Earth, our Mother, our life.

Among the Fields of Gold

Adorn your altar with corn, wheat, and corn dollies, Harvest Goddess, bread, oats, barley, squash, sickle/reap hook, Appalachian hand pictures, bread, apple juice, oats, kamut, grinder, broom.

If there is a maiden, she or another participant can sweep the area.

Assign two people as gatekeepers.

Smudge/ anoint.

Circle up.

Officiant: welcome/housekeeping, bathroom, food, sign up for temple emails, phones off, introduce ourselves and helpers.

Announcement of Temple: Friends, the temple is about to be erected and the circle cast. Let those who desire attendance gather now to prepare our sacred space. Let none be here but of their own free will.

Cast the Circle

I conjure here a circle of power, a sacred and intentional space for worship and celebration, a meeting place of joy and love and truth, a boundary between the world of humanity and the realms of the shining ones.

With steel I set a guardian and protection that shall preserve and contain the power that we shall raise within thee. This I will, in the name of the people. Wherefore do I consecrate this temple in the name of great Tailtiu and of our own Tahkeeostee and beloved Tonatzin. May we all blessed be.

North: In this time of the grain harvest, I call the Ancestors and the Guardians of the North with the strength of oats! I remember how the seed heads, tanned from the sun, stand in the wide fields near the river. I remember the threshing of the grain and the stretching stomachs it fills. I remember the bowl, with butter and sugar, and a man dressed as a friend. Hail and welcome to our table!

East: In this time of the grain harvest, I call the Ancestors and Guardians of the East with the bright yellow kernels of corn! I have planted the flat kernels in mounds the width of my hand. I have seen the shocking green of the stalks as they rise. The oldest peoples put a fish's head in the mound to feed the proud, tall spears that hold the other sister. Hail and welcome to our table!

South: In this time of the grain harvest, I call the Ancestors and Guardians of the South with the banked fire of wheat! I sing now of the fire of the sun, of the loaf made edible through the flailing of the grain. I sing now of the bright fire of food that is enduring, of food that is beautiful to see. I sing of grains that feed the people and straw that makes the bricks. Hail and welcome to our table!

West: In this time of the grain harvest, I call the Ancestors and Guardians of the West with the perfect jewels of barley! I create a necklace of the pearls of barley. I create soup from the waters of the sea and the tears of my kindred, who passed into the West. I create the living vision of a shining new world. I create a passageway for my descendants to greet my ancestors. Hail and welcome to our table!

Centering—Invocation of Tailtiu

> *Come, Beautiful Mother*
> *Come, Loving Grandmother*
> *Come, Happy Sister*
> *Join our dance,*
> *Sing with us our song.*

Thank you!
For the harvest, for the rain,
for the love.
Thank you!
Thank you!
Go raibh maith agat
do fomhar, do baisteach, do gra.

And so our circle is cast.

Explain ritual.

What have you cleared with brute strength? When have you done something the hard way? Why? Consider how we engage with famine in the world, tell the story of Tailtiu clearing the land. Ask the gathered people to remember that a sacred fast day can be a powerful spiritual practice.

The priestesses pass a plate of bread and a cup of apple juice. Participants are invited to dip the bread into the apple juice in the Ceremony of Cakes and Ale.

The priestesses bless each participant with "May you never hunger" when they take a bit of bread and "May you never thirst" when the cup is passed.

The priestesses walk around the circle widdershins with a sword.

Devocation

Go with thanks and go with blessing, Sweet Lady of the gardens, Lady of the pastures, Lady of the orchards. Or stay, for you are in our hearts always.

West: Sweet pearls, rich grain. Barley of my people. Though our circle be open, we honor the West! Blessed Grandmothers, ere you depart for your sweet and blessed realms, we bid you hail and farewell!

South: Bread-maker, brick-maker, wheat of the plains. Though our circle be open, we honor the South! Beloved Grandmothers, ere you depart for your sweet and blessed realms, we bid you hail and farewell!

East: The tall sister, the one who stands, silk and husk of corn. Though our circle be open, we honor the East! Beloved Grandmothers, ere you depart for your sweet and blessed realms, we bid you hail and farewell!

North: Tanned for the harvest, sweet beyond measure. Oats for our bellies. Though our circle be open, we honor the North! Beloved Grandmothers, ere you depart for your sweet and blessed realms, we bid you hail and farewell!

All speak for closing of circle: The circle is open but never again broken. May the Goddess fill all hearts as the grains of autumn come to harvest. Merry meet and merry part! And merry meet again!

Imbolc Ritual

Smudging and Anointing. While outside, smudge participants with turf and anoint with ice.

Turas, processing in singing "Gold Red Woman."

Welcome.

Temple talk.

Raise the Circle.

Invocation of Directions

North: Ragged breath of frost fills the lungs. Ground hard as granite, ice like iron, we stand among the great stones, still in the birth time of the new and startled world. Creatures of the oldest queen, grandchildren of the fiercest granddam, we stand in your grace. Cailleach, ancient mother, be welcome to our Imbolc rite. Welcome!

East: On the dawning air, we watch it rise—rose of poetry, gold and red. Honeyed petals of song and thorns of grief, we listen on the ridgeline in the birth time of the new and awaited world. The keening sounds. The round drums rejoice, blessed Brid on this your day! Spirits of the Bride—Goddess and Saint—wonder-working, steel—forging Brigid, be welcome to our Imbolc rite. Welcome!

South: The liquid flames rise high, devouring all they touch. See their brightness—cutting like sword through all that is spent. See Her there in shadow of flame, at the birth time of the new and bloodied world—the reddened queen, the raven chieftain, Morrighan who haunts the field. Omen crows ride with Her. Great Queen, shrewd and cunning, you are welcome to our Imbolc rite. Welcome!

West: The heavy mist gives way to rain, mirrored drops alight on the web of all life, renewing. Mother Danu gave Her name to the ambling river. Gives herself to the deepness of sea, here in the birth time of the new and briny world. Danu, mother, guide our ships as we navigate unknowable waters. Wise and strong, Danu, you are welcome to our Imbolc rite. Welcome!

Invocation

> *Brigid, Maiden, Goddess of waters' healing balm*
> *Bring us peace in this place of suffering*
> *Lend us strength and calm*
> *Mother of Earth and life*
> *Bless us with compassion and renewal*
> *In these dark times*
> *Victorious warrior woman*
> *Of the shining spear*
> *Spread your mantle of protection*
> *Over all of us here*

Charge.

All: Hear now the words of the Goddess.

I, who am the beauty of the green earth and the white moon among the stars and the mysteries of the waters, I call on your soul to rise and come to me. For I am that which gives life to the universe. I am that which turns the Great Wheel. From me all things proceed, and unto me they must return. Let my worship be in the heart that rejoices, remembering that all acts of love and pleasure are my rituals. Let there be beauty and strength, power and compassion, honor and humility, mirth and reverence within you. And you who seek to know me, know that your seeking will be useless, unless you know the mystery of that which you seek, you cannot find within your own heart, you will never find it outside yourself. For I have been with you from the beginning, my child, my self. I am the rapture and peace attained at the end of desire.

Poem.

Instruct participants on aspects and history of Brigid.

Working: Cloutie tying/girdling, candle lighting, milk pouring and healing station on side altars.

Cakes and Ale.

Candles shared and smoored.

Smooring the Fire.

Brigid Bright Arrow
To save, to shield, to surround
The hearth, the house, the household
This eve, this night, oh! This eve, this night
and every night.
Every single night.

Opening the Circle.

West: Grandmothers of the West, go if you must. But lend us your light a while longer, if you will. So may it be.

South: Grandmothers of the South, go if you must. But lend us your warmth on this cold night a while longer, if you will. So may it be.

East: Grandmothers of the East, go if you must. But lend us your scent of freedom a while longer, if you will. So may it be.

North: Grandmothers of the North, go if you must. But lend us a moment longer of grace, if you will. So may it be.

Devocation

Lady of the Sacred Flame, as we leave this circle give us strength and voice and the will to do your work. Eternal Creatrix, help us to craft our lives from the heart of our own forge, the heat and love within us spreading outward into all we do. Lady of the Holy Well, give us eyes that see true and hands that offer help lovingly, in honor of you.

Words for the Leaving/Benediction

Bed Blessing Before Sleep

In the name of Brigid,
I stand above my pillow—
Sweetened with lavender and roses,
I stand above my pillow and I bless my head
In the name of Brigid.
I touch my blanket—
Sweetened in the fresh breezes of the morn's dawning,
I touch my blanket and I bless my body
In the name of Brigid.
I sit upon my bed—
Sweetened with visions of bliss and good health,
I sit upon my bed and
I bless my sleeping
In the name of Brigid

As pillow comforts head,
as blanket warms body, as bed holds me safe,
in Brigid's loving spirit, I lay me down to sleep.

Invocation for Winter Solstice

Ancient and shining ones, you of the hidden doorways, Goddess of new beginnings, guardians of the mysteries of death and rebirth, we greet you in the time of your greatest power. May we be cleansed and purified, renewed as the light is renewed in the sky. May we sow seeds of love and courage and justice on the fields of our human hearts. May we see the sweet fruit of healing and strong community in our old world, in both body and spirit. Sacred ones, open the doors for all hearts and let that healing begin here, tonight. Let that healing spiral through the Web of all Being. So may it be, grandmothers and ancestors. Be welcome to our circle.

Chant for a Beltane Ritual.

Oh, do not tell the priest our plight,
Or he would call it a sin;
But—we have been out in the woods all night,
A-conjuring Summer in!
And we bring you news by word of mouth—
Good news for cattle and corn—
Now is the Sun come up from the South,
With Oak, and Ash, and Thorn!
—Rudyard Kipling, "A Tree Song"

Beltane blessing: May this season of Beltane bless you with strongest desires well met, with delicious encounters well times, with space for love and play and lust and passion. May you taste sweetness and softness, firm flesh of peach—and of lover. Blessed be the season and the summer, and blessed be all we.

BERM: HOMELY

Handfasting I

Flute Music. Officiant enters, walks to altar.
Welcome: What a beautiful day we have to celebrate
two people whom we all love so much. You've come from
so many places to be here for this tender event. We have
come together this afternoon in this special place, held in
the cupped hands of these ancient mountains and blessed
by the sweet wildness of this flowing stream, to celebrate
(Names') wedding. On their behalf, I welcome you.
Officiant lights incense at fire pit, blesses self at
water, walks back to altar to face waterfall.
Procession: Couple process in together. They do the
same as above. Bride removes her cape.
Couple faces officiant.
Flute music stops.
Officiant welcomes everyone, then raises circle,
mentioning the Fae.
North: We'll begin in the North with the great
greenness of the land in summer. Feel that heartbeat?
It is the land living within us and around us. Feel your
own heartbeat now and come into the great rhythm of
the land in summer—fertile, luscious, green of lichen
and fern, tree and moss. Spirits of this land, our land, we
honor and welcome you. Blessed be.
East: Turn with me now to the East and the sweet
scent of summer. Breathe deeply of this scent of summer.
There is river in it and composting leaves from last year's
autumn. Take in the richness of the tree breath and join
our elder kindred in welcoming the sun and the warm
and the winds of change. Spirits of this air, our air, we
honor and welcome you. Blessed be.

South: Let's face the South now and raise up the great bonfires of the season. Put your hand on your brow. Do you feel the heat that is you, the fire that courses through your blood? Close your eyes and feel the reflection of the great bonfires of old, flickering against your eyes. Welcome in the heat of summer. Spirits of this fire, our fire, we honor and welcome you. Blessed be.

West: We end our cast facing the West and calling in the summer rains. We stand so near the water—do you feel her, restless, moving away? Do you feel the sweat on your face, the moisture in your mouth? As the summer stretches her long limbs, we hope the gentle rains remember how welcome they are. Spirits of this water, our water, we honor and welcome you. Blessed be. Come back around to the North to make our circle whole.

Officiant explains unity candle: Two flames burning alone, found each other in the night, shall burn as one for all eternity.

Couple lights the candles.

Cakes and Ale

One to the other: May you never thirst or hunger for I shall be here.

Returning the vow: May you never thirst or hunger for I shall be here.

Couple drinks and eats, then speaks to each other words of love and commitment.

Officiant: Dear friends, we have come together today here in this place to celebrate the handfasting of _____. Before prenuptial agreements, Las Vegas wedding chapels, and unflattering bridesmaids dresses, a woman and a man made vows to each other in a simple, heartfelt ceremony that "fastened their hands" and made them a couple in the eyes of their kith and kindred. It was a peasant wedding, witnessed by family, friends, and the people of the village. Today you are the village as we join _____, King and Queen, Faery and Angel, to celebrate this very special day.

Blessing of the Elements

Couple is taken to or turned to each direction.

Officiant: May the blessings of Earth be upon this couple as they are wed. Grant to their union your gifts of stability, strength, and prosperity.

May the blessings of Air be upon this couple as they are wed. Grant to their union your gifts of wisdom and understanding.

May the blessings of Fire be upon this couple as they are wed. Grant to their union your gifts of love, passion, and creativity.

May the blessings of Water be upon this couple as they are wed. Grant to their union your gifts of intuition, inspiration, and flexibility.

True love has often been symbolized by a knotted cord. The knot is an elaboration on the Spiral of Life, reminding us that all living things have a beginning, an ending, and a rebirth and throughout these passages are eternal. Please take hands.

Couple joins right hands, then left hands over right.

Officiant: In tying this knot, I bind you heart to heart, soul to soul, and hand to hand. This cord is a symbol of your commitment to each other and this union. Keep it, always tied, as a precious possession and guard it well, as you guard your love.

The cord is tied and the blessing pronounced.

Officiant: May your life together be filled with wonder. May your union be blessed with the gifts of the elements: strength of mountain, clarity of air, passion of fire, flexibility of water, immortality of spirit.

Vows

Officiant: (to the first) Will you have _____ to live together in love and friendship? Will you love her, comfort her, honor her, and be true in sickness as well as health?
Answer/vows.
Officiant: (to the other) Will you have _____ to live together in love and friendship? Will you love him, comfort him, honor him, and be true in sickness as well as health?
Answer/vows.
With priestess holding the cord, the couple grasp their right hands and slip their left hands out of the knot. Cord is held by officiant.
Officiant: Therefore, I declare them, by the authority vested in me by this community and the state of NC to be wife and husband. Let all others honor them as such and respect the threshold of their house. Seal your union now with a kiss.
May the joy and harmony that surround us now continue to grow in their lives and in the lives of us all. May the Great Mother, whose names are numbered as the stars, bless us all as we go forth this day. As we congratulate our friends, let us remember the ancestors who came before us and the descendants who will come after. Walk in joy and love and depart this place in peace. Blessed be.
The broom is placed, and the couple jump over it.
Officiant opens the circle, mentioning the Fae.
West: And now our revels are ended, and we honor the Ancestors and Grandmothers of the West. Rain and

river and sweet Maywine—go if you must but stay if you will! Blessed be.

South: And now our revels are ended, and we honor the Ancestors and Grandmothers of the South. Bonfire and hearthfire and loving life-force—go if you must but stay if you will! Blessed be.

East: And now our revels are ended, and we honor the Ancestors and Grandmothers of the East. Song and wind and spirits of change—go if you must but stay if you will! Blessed be.

North: And now our revels are ended, and we honor the Ancestors and Grandmothers of the North. Deep green, warm soil, heartbeat of life—go if you must but stay if you will! Blessed be.

Handfasting II

Officiant: Dear friends, we have come together today here in this lovely place to celebrate the handfasting/ wedding of _____. Before prenuptial agreements, Las Vegas wedding chapels, and unflattering bridesmaids dresses, a woman and a man made vows to each other in a simple, heartfelt ceremony that "fastened their hands" and made them a couple in the eyes of their kith and kindred. It was a peasant wedding, witnessed by family, friends, and the people of the village. Today, you are all the village as we join _____ to celebrate this very special day.

The circle is cast.

Light candles on altar/table.

Blessing of the Elements: Couple is taken to or turned to each direction to cast the circle.

Officiant: May the blessings of Earth be upon this couple as they are wed. Grant to their union your gifts of stability, strength, and prosperity.

May the blessings of Air be upon this couple as they are wed. Grant to their union your gifts of wisdom and understanding.

May the blessings of Fire be upon this couple as they are wed. Grant to their union your gifts of love, passion, and creativity.

May the blessings of Water be upon this couple as they are wed. Grant to their union your gifts of intuition, inspiration, and flexibility.

Back to center/table/altar.

Officiant: Now we stand at the center of the circle where all things meet their opposite—male and female, light and shadow, matter and spirit—meet and become one. As a symbol of this, I offer you _____ these cakes, which represent the bounty of the earth and the richness of the harvest. From this day and throughout this union, one avenue to the sacred will be through _____. (Bride gives groom a bite of cake and says "May you never hunger" or similar words. Groom eats cake.) In the same spirit, I offer this chalice, which represents the ecstasy of communion and the oneness with all life. (Bride gives groom a sip from the chalice and says "May you never thirst" or similar words.)

From this day and throughout this union, one avenue to the sacred will be through _____. (Groom gives Bride a bite of cake and says "May you never hunger" or similar words. Bride eats cake.) In the same spirit, I offer this chalice, which represents the ecstasy of communion and the oneness with all life. (Groom gives Bride a sip from the chalice and says "May you never thirst" or similar words.)

Chalice and plate are returned to altar.

True love has often been symbolized by a knotted cord. The knot is an elaboration on the Spiral of Life, reminding us that all living things have a beginning, an ending, and a rebirth and throughout these passages are eternal. You each have a length of cord. Please tie them together now—end to end—and add your blessing and intent to the union of your friends.

They do so and bring the cord to the priestess.

Please take hands. (Couple joins right hands, then left hands over right.)

In tying this knot, I bind you heart to heart, soul to soul, and hand to hand. This cord is a symbol of your commitment to each other and this union. Keep it, always tied, as a precious possession, and guard it well, as you guard your love.

The cord is tied and the blessing pronounced.

Blessing words. These are quiet and intuitive in the moment. I speak them over your cord.

Here is the place for your words to each other. If you'd like more traditional—do you take this man, etc, let me know.

With priestess holding the cord, the couple grasp their right hands and slip their left hands out of the knot. Cord is placed on altar.

Rings are presented on the prayer book.

Ring blessings pronounced: Bless these rings that those who wear them, those who give and receive them, may be faithful to one another and live and grow together in love and peace. Blessed be.

Rings are exchanged. You may speak your own words here or I can supply some. Or you may simply put on the rings.

Blessing of the couple: May your life together be filled with wonder. May your union be blessed with the gifts of the elements: strength of mountain, clarity of air, passion of fire, flexibility of water, immortality of spirit.

Seal your union now with a kiss.

Therefore, I declare them, by the authority vested in me by the state of NC to be wife and husband. (You turn to face your friends.) Let all others honor them as such and respect the threshold of their house. (The broom is placed.)

The besom is an ancient and honorable tool, used for cleaning, for defense, for support. But the besom, the broom, is also a magical tool. And because of its usefulness, its domestic connotations and its versatility, the besom has long been a part of wedding rites. As _____ step over the broom, wish for them and with them the joys and pleasure of domestic life.

The guests can toss petals or blow kisses or bubbles as the couple take hands, step over the broom, and depart.

May the joy and harmony that surround us now continue to grow in _____ lives and in the lives of us all. May the Great Mother, whose names are numbered as the stars, bless us all as we go forth this evening. As we join _____ and _____, let us remember the ancestors who came before us and the descendants who will come after. Walk in joy and love and depart this place in peace. Blessed be.

Handfasting III

Ingathering and music.
Processional/Entrance of wedding party.
Welcome and Intention.
Officiant: What a beautiful day we have—to celebrate two people whom we all love so much. We stand together on this green, rich land—land that is lovingly tended by many hands and many hearts, and we rejoice in this day where hearts and hands will be joined in love.

Will those who are present here today surround
_____ in love, offering them the joys of your
friendship and support them in their marriage?

Crowd replies.

We are the keepers of the flame. This flame means
freedom and hope; it means passion and warmth. It
symbolizes the joining of two hearts and two families.
May the light and warmth of this flame be a symbol of
the warmth of the embrace we extend to the two people
whose union we honor today.

Bread and wine are presented.

Officiant: In token of your commitment this day,
we enter into the ancient ceremony of abundance.
As a symbol of your joining, I offer this bread, which
represents the pleasures of nourishing both body and
soul.

The couple, each to each, say, "May you never
hunger."

Officiants: Likewise I offer this chalice, which
represents all that is sweet and refreshing in our lives.

The couple, each to each, say, "May you never thirst."

Ring blessing. The rings are placed on officiant's
prayer book.

Officiant: Bless these rings that those who wear
them, those who give and receive them, may be honest
and loving to one another and live and grow together in
love and joy.

Keep true to the vows you take here today, not
because of any religious or civic law but out of a desire
to love and be loved by another person fully, without
limitation. May your home be filled with joy and may
it be a place where you both find your freedom, the
direction of your growth, and the sanctuary and respite
you need. May you explore the continents and oceans
together in harmony and peace.

Officiant: (to one) Will you have _____ to live together in love and friendship? Will you love her, comfort her, honor her, and be true in sickness as well as health?

Answer/vows.

Officiant: (to the other) Will you have _____ to live together in love and friendship? Will you love her, comfort her, honor her, and be true in sickness as well as health?

Answer/vows.

Long ago, young couples joined hands in a ritual called a handfasting. It was a peasant wedding, witnessed by the couple's kindred and the people of the village. Today we are the village as we join _____ to celebrate their union and to hold them in the circle of our affection.

True love has often been symbolized by a knotted cord. In tying this knot, I bind you heart to heart, soul to soul and hand to hand.

Each has a piece of cord that represents them, and officiant ties the cords together at this point, to use as the handfasting cord.

The couple's wrists are bound and the knot is tied.

This cord is a symbol of your commitment to each other. Keep it, always tied, as a precious possession and guard it well, as you guard your love.

Blessing of Couple

Officiant: May your life together be filled with wonder. May your union be blessed with the gifts of the elements: strength of mountain, clarity of air, passion of fire, flexibility of water, immortality of spirit.

Therefore I declare them joined in love. Let all others honor them as such and respect the threshold of their house. And by the power vested in me by this community and the state of NC, I declare them wife and husband. You may seal your union now with a kiss.

The couple kiss and finish the ceremony, walking back down the aisle hand in hand with the cord still around their hands.

Blessing on gathering.

Officiant: May the joy that surrounds us here in this garden continue to grow in _____'s lives and in the lives of us all. May we all be blessed as we go forth this day. May the richness of this earth enrich us, may the breezes be ever sweet, may acts of love and pleasure be ours always, and may the waters of life cleanse and soothe us. Let us remember the ancestors who came before us and think on the descendant who will come after. Walk in joy and love and depart this place in peace.

Baby Blessing I

Officiant casts the circle.

We honor the North, the Earth that nurtures us, the bones that give us form, and the deep and ancient force that moves the universe.

We honor the East, the air that sustains us, the wings of imagination and the gentle breezes and fierce gales of our souls.

We honor the South, the fire of life that burns within us, lightning and lava, the bonfires and hearths that mark the turning of the Great Wheel.

We honor the West, the waters that cover our planet, the rain from above us and the springs from below, the tears of our ancestors, and the blood of our kindred.

Priestess: We are gathered in this place between the worlds to welcome this new child to our circle.

All participants speak to Mother: May you have the strength of the Earth, the inspiration of the new dawn, the fierce love of the bear, and the ability to flow as the rivers flow, consistent and also gentle. May the Divine Spirit that enfolds us all guide you in your responsibilities.

Priestess: Blessed be.

Priestess anoints child and takes the baby.

Presents name.

Mother: Here is _____

All: Welcome, dear one.

Presentation to Quarters:

Little one, receive the blessings of Earth. _____, may you be strong in silence, fertile in growth, and always trust and honor your physical self.

Little one, receive the blessings of Air. _____, may you be clear of mind and strong of purpose, that you may know and fulfill your destiny.

Little one, receive the blessings of Fire. _____, may you contain the creative spark to dream with, the courage to keep your ideals, and the will to make your dreams come true.

Little one, receive the blessings of Water. _____, may you always trust your intuition and yield carefully to what must be.

Back at altar.

Priestess: May the universe smile gently upon you. May you choose your path wisely and walk it well. May you be gentle and strong, loving and wise. And may you be happy, for the world is good.

Response: Blessed be.

All: May you always have plenty. May you always be happy. May you always be true.

Cakes and Ale.

Benediction

May the joy that surrounds us here in this circle continue to grow in _____'s life and in the lives of us all. May the Great Mother, whose names are numbered as the stars, bless us all as we go forth this day. May the richness of this earth enrich us; may the breezes be ever sweet; may love and pleasure be ours always, and may the waters of life cleanse and soothe us. Let us remember the ancestors who came before us and think on the descendants who will come after. Walk in joy and love and depart this place in peace.

Guardians of the West, go if you must; stay if you will.

Guardians of the South, go if you must; stay if you will.

Guardians of the East, go if you must; stay if you will.

Guardians of the North, go if you must; stay if you will.

The circle is open but never again broken. May the Goddess awaken in every heart. Merry meet, merry part, and merry meet again.

All: Blessed be.

Baby Blessing II

Priestess casts the circle.

We honor the North: the Earth that nurtures us, the bones that give us form, and the deep and ancient force that moves the universe.

We honor the East: the Air that sustains us, the wings of imagination and the gentle breezes and fierce gales of our souls.

We honor the South: the Fire of life that burns within us, lightning and lava, the bonfires and hearths that mark the turning of the Great Wheel.

We honor the West: the Waters that cover our planet, the rain from above us and the springs from below, the tears of our ancestors, and the blood of our kindred.

Priestess: We are gathered in this place between the worlds to welcome this new child to the circle of love that is this family. A child is a blessing and also a responsibility, a joy as well as a concern.

(Parents' names) bear the greatest responsibility, but we who stand with them today acknowledge our place in the support and raising of this amazing person, this _____. Today in the presence of the Gods and within this circle, she also takes her place in the infinite spiral of Progenitors.

Response: Blessed be.

Priestess: (Parents' names), your love has become manifest in this perfect child. At this time of harvest, tell us what it is like to be the mother of _____.

Mother speaks.

Priestess: And _____? How is it to be her father?

Father speaks.

Priestess lays her hands on the parents.

Priestess: May you have the strength of the Earth, the inspiration of the new dawn, the fierce love of the bear, and the ability to flow as the rivers flow, consistent and also gentle. May the Divine Spirit that enfolds us all guide you in your responsibilities.

Response: Blessed be.

Priestess anoints child and takes the baby. Presents name.

Priestess: Here is (full name).

Priestess presents the baby to the quarters.

Little one, receive the blessings of Earth. _____, may you be strong in silence, fertile in growth, and always trust and honor your physical self.

Little one, receive the blessings of Air. _____, may you be clear of mind and strong of purpose, that you may know and fulfill your destiny.

Little one, receive the blessings of Fire. _____, may you contain the creative spark to dream with, the courage to keep your ideals, and the will to make your dreams come true.

Little one, receive the blessings of Water. _____, may you always trust your intuition and yield carefully to what must be.

Priestess returns to the altar.

Priestess: May the universe smile gently upon you. May you choose your path wisely and walk it well. May you be gentle and strong, loving and wise. And may you be happy, for the world is good.

Response: Blessed be.

The baby passes among the circle (carried by a parent) and is given verbal blessings from those assembled. She returns to the altar where she is given a taste of three liquids.

Priestess: (Milk) May you always have plenty. (Wine) May you always be happy. (Water) May you always be true.

Cakes and Ale.

Benediction.

Guardians of the West, go if you must; stay if you will.

Guardians of the South, go if you must; stay if you will.

Guardians of the East, go if you must; stay if you will.

Guardians of the North, go if you must; stay if you will.

The circle is open but never again broken. May the Goddess awaken in every heart. Merry meet, merry part, and merry meet again.

All: Blessed be.

House Blessing

Cornmeal and candy are given to the household spirits and the spirits of the land. Priestess passes among the guests with a bowl of scented water, and guests dip their fingers in the water.

Invocation

Ancient and shining ones, honored ancestors and beloved Long Dead, be present with us and bestow your kindest blessings on _____'s home.

Bless this house, wherein he dwells. Bless every fireside, every wall and door. Bless every heart that beats beneath its roof, every hand that toils to bring joy and every foot that crosses the peaceful threshold of this good house.

May the blessing of the Earth be upon this house— the great round Earth that nourishes us. And may the winds be kind and the harvest full.

Priestess presents salt, honey, and bread.

May this salt remind us to savor the goodness of life under this roof and under the vault of the great sky. May this honey lend its sweetness to life within these walls. May this bread bring true friends and relations and give you the opportunity to offer both hospitality and courtesy. May those within these walls remember the Ancestors who came before us and the descendants who will come after. May the household spirits and the spirits of the land be helpful and joyous, and may all those who cross the threshold of this good home do so in love and honor and depart its door in peace.

For we are all part of the deep and ancient force that flows through all things.

Blessed be.

Handparting Ceremony

Cast circle.

Officiant: We are gathered here in the sight of the Goddess to mark a difficult passage. _____ has ended a relationship and is moving forward.

Is this why you are here?

(Response.)

Do you bring with you any symbols of the union that you are dissolving?

(Response.)

What lies in the future is guided by today's visions, today's choices. What is, is. What was is now past.

Moving forward—and setting your intentions for the future—will be more easily achieved if you lighten your burden here. Clear the way before, by leaving the past where it truly belongs.

(Two candles are lit.)

This relationship was made of two people. Now these people have separated and the relationship is at an end.

(Officiant steps away from the altar with one lit candle and blows it out.)

Can you say now that this is over, that it is well and truly in the past, a part of your history, not your present?

(Response.)

Berm: Dedications and Special Ceremonies

Mother Grove Goddess Temple has a small chapel, and we dedicated it in the early months of our existence. We cleaned the space thoroughly, decorated the space with flowers, lit candles and incense. We went outside and processed in, singing and ringing bells. We rang bells throughout the space and spoke this adaptation of one of the hymns to Inanna. And when it was completed, we drank some red wine and ate some good chocolate. Believe me when I tell you that I realize how fortunate we are to have a dedicated ritual space, as well as a community that supports it.

Prayer to Inanna at the Dedication of the New Temple

As the silky darkness veils the land, the Most Radiant, the Great Light flashes Her eyes in the dark sky, the Queen of Evening appears in the arc of the night. Inanna, Great Bull of Heaven! You are the morning and the evening star. I whisper, "Hail!" to the Holy One, who appears in the heavens! I sing, "Hail!" to the Holy Priestess of Heaven! I chant aloud in the smoke of incense, "Hail!" Inanna, Queen of Heaven! As we cross the threshold into your house, I weep to carry you forth. Drunk with your fire, I whisper, you who fill the sky with light! You who brighten the day at dawn! Bless us, your daughters. Bless me, your loving priestess. I say, "Hail!" to Inanna, Great Lady of Heaven! Awesome Lady of the Annuna Gods! Crowned with curving moonlike horns, You fill the heavens and earth with light! I say, "Hail!" to Inanna, First Daughter of the Moon! Stern, ageless, timeless, as the moon is this. Swept by rain, robed in snow, green in the season, as the Earth is this. You are the morning and the evening star. Your glory known by all in heaven and on Earth and in the Great Below, Your mysteries known only to your dearest ones—your sisters, your servants, your priestesses. I whisper, "Hail!" to the Holy One, who appears in the heavens!

—A Prayer of Enheduanna, the Eldest Priestess, as transcribed through her servant.

Tree Planting Ceremony

(Before planting.)

May this tree remind us of these friends whom we love and who are now part of the circle of Ancestors. May this tree dig deep roots and grow healing branches as our community grows and flourishes through trust and love.

(After planting.)

May you have dew for a blessing and abundant rain and water for all the green and growing things, every plant and tree. And this witch hazel that we plant this day in the season of Samhain, make deep its roots and wide its crown, that it may blossom in its season and bring forth shade and fruit. For goodness and for beauty and for the memory of those who have passed the veil and made the transition from matter to spirit. We ask the Ancient Ones to strengthen our hands and our backs and give us hearts to revive the sacred soil, our oldest Mother.

So mote it be. Blessed be.

BERM: HELPFUL BITS AND PIECES

I often speak at Unitarian Universalist churches, and they are always a welcoming group. A feature of most UU services is the lighting of the ceremonial chalice, a central feature of the religion. I like to write new ones, rather than rely on the ones in the hymnal.

This section has some of those and some benedictions. Bits and pieces in case you need a quick blessing or benediction.

Benediction

The sun has set, and we sit at the threshold of the longest night of the year. I think fear may be the most contagious disease of all. More contagious than grace or courage, it seems so easy for us to fall prey to a fear that isn't even our own. When we are faced with events like inexplicable tragedy, we are invited through the bad news and disruptions, through the mourning and the anger, to engage not only life but our own lives and those beings whose lives touch ours.

As we leave this soft and solemn place, let us reconnect with the power that both is and runs the universe. Let us learn from the ancient knowing of the landscape and continue this journey to the deepest parts of our collective heritage and our own being. Let us set aside fear and sit together by the symbolic fire of our shared experience, our shared humanity, our shared life-force.

May we all blessed be.

Invocation of the Goddesses: Persephone, Demeter, and Rhea

Speaker One: Up come the greenlings, the chickweed, the dandelions.

All three speak: We sing of the Daughter, the Mother, the Mother of the Mother.

Speaker Two: As we welcome the new growing season.

Speaker One: And ponder the fullness of this sacred moon.

Speaker Three: We invoke and call forth.

Speaker Three: Persephone.

Speaker Two: Demeter.

Speaker One: Rhea.

All three speak: The triply aspected bringers of the springtime. The bringers of life.

Speaker One: Rhea.

Speaker Two: Demeter.

Speaker Three: Persephone.

All three speak: We sing of the Daughter, the Mother, the Mother of the Mother. We invite you to this our sacred circle.

Devocation

All three: Our song is done, and now we dance in your honor, bringers of spring, bringers of life. From Water, to Fire, to Air, to Earth—we dance the circle of no beginning and no ending. Blessed be!

Chalice Lighting I

Who can strike the fire from stone? Blessed is the new fire. In this season of deep rest and holy darkness, we light our chalice in expectation of returning, in celebration of things fresh and new, in memory of those who have gone before us into the West, into the realm of our ancestors. Blessed is the new fire. We gather our soul-selves around this small and mobile flame, and it kindles within us a renewal of our own commitment, our own covenant—to justice and goodness, to gratitude and hospitality. Blessed is the new fire.

Chalice Lighting II

What do we light in this simple ceremony of fire and candle? Tiny flames up here call to the flame within each of us. Dwell a moment with your own flame. Some are alight for justice, some for equality, some here for community and many for the land around us—hill and hollow, river and stone. This little light of yours and yours and mine? We renew our bonds and our vows each time this chalice is lit. Flame calls to flame, and a new world is born.

The following pieces were used to evoke the tone of individual rituals at a women's spirituality gathering. You may find them useful in your community meditations.

The Night

Night is the time when we dream and receive visions, when we rest, when we go inward in search of our personal mysteries. We step into this time of deep knowing with our souls alert for wisdom in all things, times, beings. As priestesses of the Goddess, we have special duties at this time—to dream, to honor the dark, to tend the sacred fires.

The Dawn

It is morning in our spirits, and we greet it as wise women who have been through the night. Dawn is the time of infinite possibilities, of new soft light, of greeting and remembrance. The seeds that are sown in the dark now sprout and green the world, our beloved Gaia. We step proudly into the new world that we have birthed, and we see that it is good.

The Dusk

Dusk is the transitional, liminal time—neither day or night, when anything is possible. In the dusk we make our transition from our workaday lives to sacred precinct. We leave our old roles behind as we honor and invoke our priestess selves.

☙❧

These are some tools for the work you do as a community weaver in a world that feels increasingly unwoven. There are many other tools for our work, and I hope you will seek those out too and put them to good use. We spend so much time thinking and fretting and fearing change, when it is one of the few constants. I sometimes liken it to whitewater rapids where you can't look back over your shoulder but must focus your intention on what is to come and to, in the words of Henry Wadsworth Longfellow, let the dead past bury its dead.

But we are hoarders, we humans with our scarred old chocolate boxes of memories and traumas. I think we can let the past inform us in our work, without us being so beholden to it that we can't move our heavy feet forward.

You needn't be alone in this. You can invite one or two or twenty or a thousand people to join you in creating these cultural transitory artworks.

We need you, we hungry and lost beings. We need you to be brave and silly. We need you to sing us—and dance us—home.

"...let us then be up and doing, with a heart for any fate; still achieving, still pursuing, learn to labor and to wait."

—Longfellow, "A Psalm of Life."

People often ask me how long this "Tower Time" thing is going to last, as though it is an astrological occurrence of known duration, like the oft-dreaded Mercury in retrograde. I don't know. I have no idea how long it takes to transform cultures that resist healthy change, indeed any change that isn't driven by planned obsolescence or product branding. Will I see the "end" of it? Unlikely. Will there be an "end"?

No. We will segue into the new things and add them into some of the old things, and then we will move on. There will be markers on the way—some dramatic, some hardly noticeable. But a century from now, people will look back on these challenging times and shake their heads that we were so naïve or fearful or venal.

None of that will be correct.

All of it will be.

We are not servants to either the past or the future. Our work belongs here in the present in this beautiful and devastated place, where we are balancing the chaos of changing seasons, of cycles cycling, of the agricultural year taking her curtain call. Aside from this Tower Time business, we are beset with a thousand troubles and a truckload of grief and guilt. Have you tended your altar and prayed? Have you listened for the voices of your Ancestors and beloved dead? Heed what they tell you.

Gather those you love to you—even if you have to use Skype or Google Hangout—and really listen to each other. Let the Wild Hunt pass over and away from you and give the Divines a break from your incessant need. Turn to your tribe for warmth and companionship, as well as cookies and hard cider.

Remember to breathe deeply, to drink good water, to hold those you love close to your bosom. Strategize, love deeply, practice resilience. You know what the next part is. I know you do.

Fear not, friends. Fear not. Because the season is sharp and deep.

Winter has come. It's Tower Time.

ADDENDUM

This is the entire Tower Time document file as it appears on my blog. Parts of it appear elsewhere in this book. I have added it here in its entirety for easy reference.

The Tower Time Documents Prologue

This may seem like a bit of an anticlimax after all these years of warnings and thoughts and predictions about this Tower Time business. I've decided to create thematic documents so I can add information as it comes up or as experiences should be recorded. I hope these are helpful to you as we navigate the times that are our times. So please consider this a first edition.

A Knowing, Cassandra-like

I feel I owe you all a slightly more thorough explanation of "Tower Time," a phrase I have been using somewhat cavalierly for a decade or more and one which I find myself using with increasing frequency.

I don't remember precisely when it began, this quiet knowing that has grown, for me into a certainty. It began with a pinch of insight, a glint of what was happening globally reflected in local events. It was more than a lack of harmony, of simple chaotic modern life—this feeling hinted at larger activity, a shift in the zeitgeist, a disturbance in the force.

This early knowing pointed obliquely to the old dream of every old feminist—the Collapse of the Patriarchy. Since our fiercer days in the long-ago 1970s, many of us have modified our speech—often because people refuse to understand that patriarchy is a system or a set of systems and is not merely angry women being mad at and blaming men. We now talk about Hierarchical, Top-Down Systems—HT-DS for those of you who must have an acronym for everything—and that's the language I will use here. But for those of you who still call the patriarchy by its oldest name, you may translate HT-DS to "patriarchy" and you will be accurate.

Tower Time is named for the card in the tarot deck, of course, specifically the Smith-Waite deck (which is the one I've been reading for more than thirty years). The Tower is one of the more direct cards in any reading, and it lends itself to these times.

We—you and you and me—are living in a time of dramatic transition. The West is transitioning from the Age of Fossil Fuels, not gracefully, I might add. We as a planet are experiencing the most recent in a series of mass extinctions. We have moved into a post-Industrial Age—what the brilliant John Michael Greer calls "the deindustrial world"—where we collectively have lost the willingness to grow our own food and not piss in our water source. Whether or not you believe that the climate is changing globally through human agency is completely immaterial to me, but I believe it is occurring and we lack the political will and the political power to override the interests of business and industry (and, let's face it, the dominant culture) to mitigate that in any way.

The clear knowing that I felt has grown more insistent in the intervening years. It is this: we are living in times when these massive, ancient and toxic systems that have both created civilization as we know it and doomed it are crashing under their own weight of history and grief. It is the death throes of patriarchy that we are experiencing, and it will die as it has lived—in violence and oppression and injustice and death.

I did mention that this may be difficult to absorb, didn't I? Many people nod and express their own sense of the rightness of this information. Others refuse to believe it, pointing—quite accurately—to the many instances in history where a group of loonies has believed it is the end of the world. I won't engage in argument with you or read long reports that have come from dubious media or academic sources. This is intuitive—that is the very nature of a knowing. You are free to believe or not, as befits your sense of the current time and your knowledge of history and as that sense dictates.

Here's a thing I do know. This is the time we were made for and one of the reasons we're here. Tower Time.

Religion as empire, state as empire, education as empire, healing as empire—all are recalibrating in their individual descents. Each of us is in our personal place as the Tower erupts and crumbles. Some of us stand on the top, blissfully unaware that anything long-term is occurring below our feet. Some are trapped among the turrets, calculating a way off. Some have flown away and are gone to wherever and whatever comes after this life, after matter has become spirit. There are rock climbers who are testing hand and footholds as they work their way down the walls to perceived safety. Some are among the rocks at the base and some are out of sight, gone on to do the new work.

Because there is new work and it is past time to engage in it, our work during the collapse is to not stop there, gawking at the impending calamity. We are charged—and many people are deep into this work— with creating new systems, systems that are genuinely cooperative, nurturing, sustainable, and of greatest importance, resilient. There are groups that are forming in some areas to learn new/old skills, to get going with the new times. But they often bog down in meeting after meeting, talking through modes of governance, of how to hold a meeting without Robert's Rules. Remind them that time's a-wasting and that talk can happen while food is being planted or tended or preserved. Decisions can be made while looping rugs and milking goats. If your group is dreaming big dreams but spending most of their time arguing protocol, you made need a new group. Because it is happening now. There isn't some future Big Event that is looming on the horizon that marks the beginning. It's here.

As I sat with other gardeners around a fire a few weeks ago, I realized something. If you have been waiting for the other "shoe" to fall, for the crap to hit the fan, you can stop waiting. It's here, friends. Time's up. We are in it—whatever it is. Continue gathering your allies, holding those you love close, planning, working, playing, and thinking. But make no mistake, it's here. Tower Time. Put on your game face and keep your courage up. These are the times we were made for.

Per ardua ad terra!

Going to Ground in Tower Time

Early in the Gulf of Mexico oil well disaster—when it was apparent that the problem would not be solved quickly—a small group of women gathered in the small temple. They brought rum and watermelon, and the room soon filled with clouds of rich incense. Chants for Yemaya began softly, and rattles were gently rattled. As the spirit of despair was tamped down and the strands of joy and connection wove themselves into the singing and the smoke, the chants grew stronger. The dancing, which was little more than rhythmic stomping, began. The Beloved Crone seemed to be speaking an unknown language, as water bottles were chugged and offerings were made to Ancestors and Deities. The woman nearest the altar—the one who had issued the invitation—muttered prayers and knelt on the floor, singing the holy names. As she had promised, she flung herself full-length in front of the wooden altar and begged the sea Goddesses for mercy. The singing and chanting continued for some time until the participants were dry and tired, eyes streaming tears of grief and too much smoke.

Sometimes when we pray, we forget that prayer is not simply sending our best intention into the universe. For those of us who see the Ancestral Goddesses as incorporeal beings who have some authority and ability in the world, the prayers and the singing honor Beloved Ones who are near us but are not us. The invocations in which we implore them to fix our lives or clean up our messes or show us a way through are requests and bargainings. We understand that we have a part in this relationship, but we do not have control. We are not the boss. We are participants in an ancient cycle of creation and destruction and re-creation.

And sometimes the answer is no. Sometimes the answer is—you got yourself into this and you and your people are going to have to fix what you broke. You are going to have to take personal responsibility and get yourselves out of it.

Our community was far away from the horror and ineptitude that was the Gulf disaster, high in the southern mountains. But we are none of us "away," are we? We are all connected—physically, spiritually, and electronically. We know that today's oil slick is picked up by next month's hurricane and deposited in our organic gardens, on our longed-for heirloom tomatoes.

We work ourselves into a frenzy of grief and guilt and spiritual activity. We open ourselves to the sorrow and anger and filter it as best we can. We meet for coffee and walks, and we talk for hours on the phone. Gentling the community in its outrage, cushioning it from outright despair. We are blown about by the winds and waves of all that assails us, and sometimes the only place to go for succor, for comfort, is away from the computer and the phone and the endless cups of coffee. To the garden, to the woods, to the earth.

There's an evocative expression that has become a keystone for my work in the community of late. The phrase "going to ground" has taken on new significance as we stand in this challenging Tower Time. To "go to ground" is to run pell-mell back to the den or burrow, to find someplace safe to hide. To make a run for it. Foxes do it. Rabbits do it.

Since the earthquakes that ripped through Haiti in January of 2010, there has been a series of human-made and natural disasters that have been unremitting in their intensity, and we have been subsumed in the wake of them.

How many times have I forgotten—forgotten!— the people of Nashville, TN, who were inundated literally with the rising waters of the Cumberland. The seaquake and tsunami and the ongoing nuclear tragedy in Japan sets on already-heavy hearts. There have been storms and volcanoes, floods and bombers. One after another, a laundry list of devastation that can barely be acknowledged, much less comprehended.

In my community work, in my social networking, in counseling seekers with Mother Grove congregants, I have been calling the times in which we move Tower Time. I imagine that the vast foundations are cracking and we are in the top of the Tower, where we must leap outward or be crushed with the weight of this six-thousand-year-old system in its death throes.

Tower Time—we must engage or perish. We cannot remain untouched, uninvolved, because it does involve us. All of us. But the overwhelming-ness of it—how do we find the wings to fly from the Tower? How do we glide away from the mess and the pain and not look back to those falling faster and faster?

We don't. We can't. It is not in our nature. And so we bear the wounds and we keep on, even as we feel the spiritual lifeblood leaking out, only to be replaced by ennui and despair. In our circles, we call for "grounding." We speak the words of guided meditations in which roots grow from our feet and sink, gratefully, into the earth.

Grounding. Going to ground.

We are furry mammals, warm animals, wounded animals. We have tried to think ourselves out of this mess. We've tried to ritualize ourselves out of this mess. But you know what a wounded animal does. A rabbit or groundhog or badger? They go to ground and lick their wounds. They hide in their burrow, in the very womb of the earth and they take time to heal and regroup.

I'm not suggesting we bury our heads in the sand, that we run away from our spiritual responsibilities. I'm advising that when the going gets too much for you to bear, you remember that you are a warm animal and you have a special option because of that. You can go to your burrow to recuperate and lick your wounds. Then you can return to your community renewed as the clever and powerful badger that you are.

Finally, here's my advice to a friend who was feeling ungrounded, displaced, abandoned by Goddess and community. I offer it here for you, with a few additions and points of clarification, if you have need of grounding. Here is a too-brief checklist of possibilities if you are finding yourself in the midst of the falling Tower, unable to do more than gasp as the earth rises to meet you.

Have you set an energy trap?

Have you set wards? Are your shields up? If you can't do that, let your community know and they will shield you until you can.

How is your altar?

Go out to your land and ask for help. Invoke your ancestors and the land spirits. Take an offering. Bring some of the dirt in with you. Put it in your pockets, on your altar.

Brick dust at the secondary entrances to the house—windows, back door, crawl space door. Not a line, just a drop.

White dust at the front door—can even be baking soda. Salt works too.

Light a rue candle, if you have one.

Spend time outside, sitting on the dear old Earth.

Invite others to join you in a simple ritual of healing and grounding.

The best advice I have is "go to ground." Earth everywhere. Dirt, dirt. Then evaluate and see where you are.

Go to ground, sisters and brothers. Earth everywhere. It's Tower Time.

Cardinal Cross in Tower Time

My friend Diotima is an extraordinary astrologer. See, I know enough about astrology to be dangerous, and the rest of it sounds like adults in those Peanuts shows—wah, wah, wah. She somehow makes it make sense, even to me.

Here's her take on where we are right now:

http://witchesandpagans.com/Pagan-Culture-Blogs/heartbleed-hotel.html

The world is an awfully ragged place to me right now, friends. The UN recently released an official report on the rate of global climate change, and it isn't a pretty thing. And has seemingly been met with the usual tepid response by The Powers That Are.

We're still looking for that Malaysian airliner. We're still digging bodies out of the mudslide.

The garden is planted a bit and things are rising up—spinach, kale, chard, potatoes, onions, cukes, lettuces of several sorts. The recent cold snap—what we call dogwood winter around here—bit the taters, but everything else is fine. The apple trees are in full and fabulous bloom—including the new espaliered Stayman Winesap. The violets are luxurious, the dandelions crisp and delicious.

But this Cardinal Cross has combined with this Tower Time, and it is hard to shake the sadness some days.

The ferry in Korea has split my heart, I fear. All those children, those parents, the stern and unyielding sea. I haven't yet been able to wrap any sort of cord around the breakingness of my heart around this. I am anxious for news and yet completely without hope. I can't imagine what it will be like when they get the cranes in place and pull the ferry upright. I can't imagine what that scene will be like—how hard that job will be, how impossible it will be to endure for those parents who are waiting, waiting.

So... per usual... I am sinking my knees into the earth, the good rich soil of my land here. I am smelling apple blossoms and counting peony budlets. I am not doing much writing, but I am spending time at my home altar, wondering. I am wistful about the coming Beltane with its magic and whimsy.

Because we are sitting on the horns of a great shifting of our culture, and we all must find the ways to hold on, to create beauty, to be kind to one another, and to hold space for the grief and the hunger.

Viva! in the Time of the Dead

We began a discussion on Facebook, as one does, about the nature of societal change and the onset of the much-discussed revolution. I had just gotten up from a long nap and gathered my haunted thoughts and replied.

I talk about Tower Time rather a lot and people always ask—when is that going to happen? It is happening now, and I think Tower Time and the elusive revolution we've all been longing for (but are also a little afraid of) is also ongoing. I take much of my information about how to be in the world from nature (not surprising since I'm a Pagan), and this time we are in will have earthquakes and tremors and landslips and landslides. We need to reenvision what "revolution" looks like because it won't be several "important" actions, then skirmishes until the goal is achieved. This is tectonic and will take time.

Natural, incremental.

Unstoppable.

It's here; we're in it. Time for deep thinking, lateral thinking, vision.

These are the Times We are Made for... No, Really

We are all subject to the dramas and disasters that seem to abound in this moment in time. As always, I ask that you breathe deeply, ground yourself.

There. Marginally better? Good.

I have been dispensing my particular—some would say peculiar—brand of calming advice over on Facebook, and I'm simply reposting some of it here.

Take a deep breath, friends. Ground yourself into the bosom of the earth. Now, from this place of strength and relative safety, open your heart to those in need of your goodness, your strength. Speak gentle words to those who need them... and kick the asses of those that need that too.

The world is aswirl with chaotic energy right now. We always have choices then, but the two obvious ones are ground and hold—or ride the chaos. What we do tends to be determined by how strong we feel at the moment. Going to ground like a little furry critter is always a good option.

With respect and love to my colleagues... the system can't be overhauled. The system has to be uprooted, turfed out, composted so that its rot will feed the new system. We have tinkered around the edges for far too long.

In this time of grief and fear and fury, it has been a comfort to sit with my own past and with the magic of my forebears. Blessed be the ancestors! May they stand with their descendants and bring us wisdom, strength, vision.

It is neither the one thing nor the other, friends. Breathe, ground, if you can. You can stand in solidarity while lamenting the burning of the city. You can hold many emotions at the same time or sequentially—fear, fury, grief, longing. You can feel traumatized and triumphant. This is complicated, this time of change and growth. You are free to feel what you need to feel as you sort through the events in our world.

In this case—unlike Watts in 1965 and Baltimore in 1968—we are the seeds that are awakened by fire. It's up to us to go into the forest that is Baltimore and Ferguson and Pine Ridge and Oceana, and bring the green. What is left when things are cleared away? The people who are dreaming/weaving/scheming these new systems have to be at the tables of power that will gather now. They/we must demand real change—not overpaid consultants, not political platitudes. Those people are already working in those places and we—from afar—can help them feel their own authority to initiate real change. The people on the ground in all those places have been told to be patient, let the system work, calm down, wait. What is happening now is that the real people who live real lives in those real places have reached the perfect point of despair. Some of us have been there too—and it would have taken only that rush of clear destructive energy to bring the change. Certainly there are other ways to achieve change, but they are intentionally hobbled by so many things so deeply ingrained in our culture. It is worth it—thinking this through, being articulate. Because it won't stop in Baltimore or Ferguson or NY.

Sometimes what we are doing is kindling past the apathy of culture and life. Sometimes we are lighting signal fires to let the next generation know that we care about the world we are leaving to them. Sometimes fire is light, sometimes it is heat, always in its wake—there is renewed life. I always take nature as my teacher, and I think about forest fires—the terror, the destruction, and the aftermath of livid green. It is all a cycle, you know. The Great Cycle. Creation/Destruction/Creation.

So if you are overwhelmed with a desire to help, look at your community and see if there are people who are hungry—because they are there. Look to see if there is land that needs protection—because there is. You can help. You can feel. It's okay to do both. Think of your friends and colleagues who have been triggered by recent events—check in with them. Check in with the people who are always strong but now are quiet. Send them your good love and attention.

That's all for today. Except this:

Fear not. Fear not.

Beginning... From Here

What if you chose to be proactive in this Tower Time of ours? What if we—each of us—simply said enough is enough? There's a truism in the nonprofit world about tackling a big, complicated problem: "How do you eat an elephant? One bite at a time." Let's take a bite, together, to secure our resilience in these chaotic times. A tiny step into freedom from fear, a wee dance step into the circle we all long to create. Today, right now, I am going to my altar (in the middle of the day!) and am saying a word or two to themselves. Time to fly, sisters and brothers. We have been too long looking down, fearing the day. We don't have time to dillydally or fret about things we can't fix. Time to figure out what needs fixing and see if we have the tools to do it. I suspect we do. Shall we?

Chop Apples, Carry Compost—a Farmer's Meditation

Chopping apples became a meditation for me today. The kitchen was set up with various cutting boards, colanders, and stainless steel bowls, and a large pot in the sink held water to wash the apples. I started this morning by sharpening two of my favorite knives. Porch to kitchen. Wash and drain. Chop, chop, chop. Refuse to the compost tub. Chops into bags. Repeat.

It gave me time to clear the noise of this past couple of weeks out of my head. Chop, chop, chop. I was standing at my kitchen workstation and began to wiggle my feet and sway as I chopped. A little tune came into my head and I hummed as I worked.

Chop, chop, chop.

And because I was standing, I took time to do a good deep grounding and check in with the good Earth. A cool, damp breeze drifted in the open window. I let the feel of it cool my back and my soul a bit too. These are complicated days to try to think through and impossible days to try to sort out feelings in. So I let my heart drift too—I left Charleston behind and Sudan and Greece and the red wolves and the damaged Gulf. I felt it flow down into the good earth to become compost for this new world we're building.

I think about—too much about—resilience these days. As all these systems collapse, as we learn to navigate by the stars and the sun in Tower Time, what does it mean to love the land while looking askance at the people—my species—who inhabit it? Resilience, survival. Community and food and caring and love.

Chop, chop, chop.

There is so much visible pain, so many angry fearful people, and I have been angry and frustrated and fearful myself in these days. But this day of simple, monotonous work and the gift of grounding have brought me some healing, I think. And some remembering of who I am and where I am.

As we approach this flawed nation's birthday, what are you remembering? How are you healing yourself, your community, and the souls you hold dear.

Chop, chop, chop.

May we all remember well, friends. Even those of us who have named it are not immune to the stresses and chaos of Tower Time.

Lighting Signal Fires in Tower Time

I've written rather a lot about Tower Time. For Cassandra figures like me, there is nothing satisfying about seeing visions come to fruition. We are experiencing the roiling change, the fear, the uncertainty that is almost programmatic in this enormous shift. Many communities are easily seen to be in peril, but I say to you that all communities are thus.

Yes, the veil is so thin as to be nonexistent, so if you are feeling your ancestors and descendants close to you, you are experiencing that. If your garden is flourishing and feels delightful, that is because it is filled with beings of delight that you can now perceive on some level. If you are not meeting with like-minded people to figure out where we as a species go from here, you had best get started. Time's a-wasting, as we say hereabouts. This world is shuddering and shifting and moving out—it is up to all of us to decide the human worlds that will inhabit this physical space.

Perhaps we can refrain from the word bombs and ego lightning and get on with the reasons we're actually here.

Something you may find helpful right now is to ground yourself deeply and shield yourself too. Do all the self-care we've been discussing ad infinitem—hydrating, exercise, nutritious food. Holding fast to the good that you are and that you know.

Remember how strong you are and what you have already been through.

We are shaky now, frightened, angry. Go to your altar and renew your daily spiritual practice. Go outside. Remember. Remember who you are and where you are and your golden wild heart. Find your tribe and sit in circle with other tribes, either literal or virtual.

A thought, in love, from your village witch.

RESOURCES

Books

Buhner, Stephen. *Sacred and Herbal Healing Beers*
Denzer, Kiko, and Hannah Field. *Build Your Own Earth Oven*
Deppe, Carol. *The Resilient Gardener*
Ehrenreich, Barbara. *Bright-Sided*
Ehrenreich, Barbara. *Dancing in the Streets*
Eisler, Riane. *The Real Wealth of Nations*
Forbes, Bronwen. *Making Merry in Step and Song*
Freeman, Charles. *AD 381*
Giles, Janice Holt. *Hannah Fowler*
Hartley, Dorothy. *Lost Country Life*
Kindred, Glennie. *Letting the Wild Edges In*
Kingsolver, Barbara. *Animal, Vegetable, Miracle*
Klein, Naomi. *Shock Doctrine*
Linde, Nels and Judy. *Taking Sacred Back*
Magliocco, Sabine. *Witching Culture*
Manchester, William. *World Lit Only By Fire*
Orr, Emma Restall. *Kissing the Hag*
Pratchett, Terry. *Wee Free Man, A Hat Full of Sky, Winter King*
Ranck, Shirley Ann. *Cakes for the Queen of Heaven*
Shaw, Martin. *Scatterlings*
Shiva, Vandana. *Earth Democracy*
Stamets, Paul. *Mycelium Running*
Starhawk. *Earth Path*
Starhawk. *The Fifth Sacred Thing*
Starhawk and M. Macha Nightmare. *The Pagan Book of Living and Dying*
Tate, Karen. *Sacred Places of Goddess*

Weber, Andreas. *Matter and Desire*

Wolkstein, Diane and Noah Kramer. *Inanna: Queen of Heaven and Earth*

Web-based Resources

Community Chickens, communitychickens.com

Mother Earth News, motherearthnews.com

Natural Building Network, nbnetwork.org

Seed Savers Exchange, seedsavers.org

ABOUT THE AUTHOR

H. Byron Ballard, BA, MFA, is a western North Carolina native, teacher, folklorist, and writer. She has served as a featured speaker and teacher at Sacred Space Conference, PantheaCon, Pagan Spirit Gathering, Southeast Wise Women's Herbal Conference, Glastonbury Goddess Conference, the Scottish Pagan Federation Conference, Mystic South, and other gatherings. She is senior priestess and cofounder of Mother Grove Goddess Temple in Asheville, NC, where she teaches religious education as well as leads rituals. She is one of the founders of the Coalition of Earth Religions/CERES, a Pagan nonprofit, and does interfaith work locally and regionally.

Her writings have appeared in print and electronic media. Her essays are featured in several anthologies, including *Birthed from Scorched Hearts* (Fulcrum Press), *Christmas Presence* (Catawba Press), *Women's Voices in Magic* (Megalithica Books), *Into the Great Below*, and *Skalded Apples* (both from Asphodel Press).

She blogs as "Asheville's Village Witch" (myvillagewitch.com) and writes a regular column for *Witches and Pagans* magazine.

Her pamphlet "Back to the Garden: a Handbook for New Pagans" has been widely distributed, and she has two books on Appalachian folk magic— *Staubs and Ditchwater: A Friendly and Useful Introduction to Hillfolks' Hoodoo* and *Asfidity and Mad-Stones: A Further Ramble through Hillfolks' Hoodoo* (Smith Bridge Press). *Embracing Willendorf: a Witch's Way of Loving Your Body to Health and Fitness* was published in April 2017 also by Smith Bridge Press. Byron is currently at work on *Gnarled Talisman:*

Old Wild Magics of the Motherland and *The Ragged Wound: Salving the Broken Spirit of Appalachia.*

Contact her at www.myvillagewitch.com or info@ myvillagewitch.com.

CPSIA information can be obtained
at www.ICGtesting.com
Printed in the USA
FFOW02n0026080718
47320083-50326FF